I0570146

时 代 梦
The Dream of an Era

A版
A Version

编剧:海

Screenwriter: HC

书名:《时代梦》
著者:海
平装本ISBN: 979-8-9914012-4-1
出版日期:2024年9月第一版
定价:$18.00美元

出版与分发机构
Asian Culture Press LLC
1942 Broadway St., Suite 314c,
Boulder, CO 80302, United States

版权声明:

为适应全球不同地区的法律法规要求,《时代梦》剧本共分为A、B、C三个版本。此次出版的A版为根据各国建议, 对涉及人性、性、暴力、敏感政治事件等内容进行删减后的版本, 旨在为广大观众呈现一部具有普世价值的作品。B版和C版将根据A版出版后的反馈情况, 以及各地区具体的法律法规要求, 陆续推出。请以中文版本为准, 英文译本仅供参考。

本剧本A版为虚构作品, 所有角色及情节均为创作虚构, 部分角色灵感来源于现实人物, 但与其实际生活无关。剧中提及的历史事件、政治人物及被定罪的罪犯名字均为真实的, 所描绘的历史背景旨在反映中国社会的变迁。

免责声明:

本剧本中的所有虚构角色及公司名称均为作者创作, 任何与现实人物、公司或事件的相似之处纯属巧合。作品中的观点、态度及立场仅代表作者个人, 不代表任何组织或机构。

前　言

————·————

征集片名！正在创作一部电影剧本，根据读者建议，拟定以下几个中文片名：

- 《时代梦》
- 《中国往事》
- 《北京往事》
- 《岁月往事》

欢迎大家留言，分享您的想法，帮助作者确定最终片名。

近来，我突然内分泌紊乱，伴有厌食症，感觉衰老了许多，起因与女性有关。

趁着我还能够行动，记忆和思维尚且清晰，我想先简单总结一下自己的一生，或许可以写一部自传。同时，我决定续写之前写到 2017 年的电影剧本《时代梦》。

这部自传并非传统意义上的"传"，因为我一生碌碌无为，一事无成，没有值得传颂的事迹。它更像是围绕着女性唤起的一些无聊记忆。

曾经，我狂妄自大，异想天开地写了电影剧本《时代梦》，并两次向 xxx 局递交剧本梗概，申请拍摄许可证，但都被驳回了。

朋友们劝我，现在国家提倡"中国梦"，我的剧本却敢用《时代梦》这个名字，简直是反了！况且，拍电影需要大量的资金投入，没有两亿人民币的预算，想都别想。即使勉强拍了，想拿到放映许可证更是难上加难，最终只会竹篮打水一场空。

于是，剧本写到 2017 年后便搁置了。

现在，我已经开始着手写自传《一生遇到的女人们》，并决定同时续写电影剧本《时代梦》。在续写之前，我将原先写的剧本梗概陆续连载发布，与大家分享。

Preface

————•————

Seeking Title Suggestions! I am currently working on a movie script and have proposed the following Chinese titles based on reader suggestions:

- *The Dream of an Era*
- *Tales of China*
- *Tales of Beijing*
- *Tales of Time*

I welcome everyone to leave comments and share your thoughts to help me decide on the final title.

Recently, I've been experiencing endocrine disorders and anorexia, making me feel significantly older. These issues seem to be related to women.

While I can still move around, with my memory and thoughts relatively clear, I want to summarize my life briefly. Perhaps I could write an autobiography. At the same time, I have decided to continue writing the movie script *"The Dream of an Era,"* which I had paused in 2017.

This autobiography is not a traditional one, as my life has been uneventful and unremarkable, lacking significant accomplishments. It is more of a collection of mundane memories, mostly revolving around women.

Once, in my arrogance, I wrote a movie script called "*The Dream of an Era*" and submitted a synopsis twice to XXX Administration of Radio, seeking a filming permit. Both attempts were rejected.

My friends advised me that with the country's current advocacy of the "Chinese Dream," my script titled "The Dream of an Era" seemed somewhat rebellious. Moreover, making a movie requires a substantial financial investment. Without a budget of at least 200 million Chinese yuan, it's hardly worth considering. Even if the movie were somehow made, obtaining a film screening license would be extremely difficult, ultimately resulting in a futile effort.

Therefore, the script was shelved after reaching the year 2017.

Now, I have begun working on my autobiography, "*The Women I Have Met in My Life*," and have decided to simultaneously continue writing the movie script, "The Dream of an Era." Before proceeding with the continuation, I will be serializing and sharing the original script synopsis with everyone.

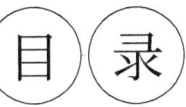 目 录

Table of Contents

《时代梦》剧本梗概

◇ 编剧：海　2017 年元月

1. 剧本简介

　　《时代梦》是一部跨越四十五年的时代剧，剧中的虚构人物是以现实人物为原型创作的。影片中的五位主角，1 女 4 男，是 1972 年北京一所小学五年级二班的同学。影片讲述了五位同学李飞、陆程、唐龙、舒晓萍、杜雄从 1972 年到 2017 年，跨越四十五年所走过的不同人生轨迹，反映了中国四十五年的社会变迁轨迹，以及与外部世界发展的相互交织，体现个人命运与时代社会发展的息息相关。

2. 剧本结构

　　影片采用两条线平行展开叙述，以中国叙述为主，美国叙述为辅，两条线相互交替贯通。影片用倒叙手法，从 1972 年尼克松访华开始叙述，一直到 2016 年奥巴马下台、特朗普当选美国总统。

3. 主要人物

3.1. 李飞: 四十五载人生历程

出身与性格

李飞成长于普通知识分子家庭，性格鲜明，傲上不欺下，仗义直言，不畏权贵，爱打抱不平。他善于观察，思想敏锐，视野开阔，经历丰富。

少年时代

作为典型北京机关大院男孩，李飞完整经历了文革七十年代后期北京的动荡。他性格叛逆，反潮流，打架斗殴，追逐女孩。与初恋女同学舒晓萍关系亲密，对外界世界充满好奇。

大学生活

1980 年，李飞考入北京 xx 学院。这所大学只招收北京本地学生，毕业生也都会留在北京工作。因此，学习毫无压力，校风也较为颓靡。李飞并未认真读过书，而是利用课余时间下广东倒卖服装电子产品，目睹了大学同学偷渡香港被遣返关押的事件。

步入社会

大学毕业后，李飞进入国企进出口公司工作，86 年开始频繁出入深圳广州，亲历了深圳股票交易所开业，参加广州交易会，并在上海、海南等地做进出口贸易。

1989 年，李飞返回对外经贸大学进修英文，期间参与了六四事件全过程，险些被枪弹击中。

闯荡商海

此后，李飞频繁来往（北美），中东海湾国家、日韩、香港、东南亚等地，经营大宗商品水泥、钢材等。九十年代初，他被公司派驻香港做首席代表，亲眼目睹了香港九七回归前后全过程。

人生历练

李飞还亲身经历并被卷入海南、湛江、福建等地进口商品走私事件，结识了赫赫有名的走私团伙赖氏集团，险些丧命于黑社会及腐败公检法机构手中。

反思与重生

1997 年，李飞从香港返回北京，又陷入国企公司内部领导争权夺利，极度失望，萌生去意。1999 年，他选择移居加拿大，游历北美大陆数年，体验不同生活和文化方式，度过一段平静生活。

2005 年，李飞返回中国重新创业，却因合伙人选择不当、决策失误，以及自身性格上的固执而导致几次商业投资未达预期。他曾参与一项新型水泥项目的投资，占有20%的股份，投产后市值到达 10 亿人民币以上，随着项目逐渐发展，市值大幅上升。然而，由于当地商业环境的复杂性和激烈的市场竞争，项目遭遇了许多法律和制度上的挑战，最终导致公司权益受到侵害。尽管经过长时间的法律争端，案件并未得到预期的结果。期间，他目睹了在激烈的市场竞争中，国有企业和民营企业为争夺资源和市场份额而采用了多种竞争手段。这段经历让他身心俱疲，深刻体会到了商业世界的艰难与不确定性。

大学最好的朋友唐龙因卷入商业诈骗案被判刑 7 年，至今还在监狱中；儿时的玩伴杜雄也因吸毒袭警毙命于狱中。这些经历让李飞最终醒悟，开始看淡名利，重新思考人生。

重拾梦想

2015 年，李飞重返加拿大，萌生创作电影剧本的想法，希望借此认真回顾四十五年成长经历，完整展现中国同期发展历程。

平凡而精彩

李飞的人生没有轰轰烈烈的事业，也没有取得非凡成绩，但他的经历贯穿于 1972 年后中国社会 45 年发展的各个历史阶段，亲身经历众多历史事件及真实人物。敏锐的观察力使他能够认真思考总结，并反映在其所创作的剧本中。

3.2. 陆程：戎马生涯

少年英才

陆程是李飞的发小，从小身材高大，体育健将，与李飞一起打架斗殴，是好友也是对手。他励志长大后成为军人，并暗恋同学舒晓萍，但一直将这份感情埋藏在心底。

军旅生涯

高中毕业后，为了减轻单相思的痛苦，陆程执意报考外地军校，实现了成为军人的理想。在军旅生涯中，他历经磨练，最终成长为一名身居要职的优秀职业军人。

经历风雨

陆程经历了从八九年的六四动荡，到中国使馆被炸、中美撞机事件、九七香港回归军队驻防、海外维和、索马里护航、钓鱼岛冲突等一系列重大事件。在这些事件中，他临危不惧，出色完成任务，为国家和人民做出了重要贡献。

中美交涉

作为中方军队代表，陆程负责与美方代表交涉，在维护国家利益方面扮演了重要角色。他与后来成为舒晓萍丈夫的美国军官大卫托马斯，因工作往来，建立了既是对手又是朋友的良好合作关系。

3.3. 唐龙：商海传奇

早年成就

唐龙，年少时便展现出非凡的商业天赋。他拥有云南王龙亲族血脉，身材高大，相貌英俊，技艺出众，是北京乒乓球少年冠军之一。与李飞为死党，共同涉足（电子），服装贸易，奠定了他在商界的基础。

商业征程

在北京和深圳的商业征途上，唐龙与李飞并肩作战，共同打拼，尝尽甜酸苦辣。他勇于冒险，曾试图偷渡香港（转到美国），但最终被截获。

风云变幻

唐龙的生活并非一帆风顺。他沉迷于酒色，经常出入私人舞会，饱受世俗诱惑。一次私人聚会导致他被捕，劳教半年并丧失学籍。尽管如此，他凭借着聪明过人、女人缘和乒乓球技艺，在家人和亲戚的帮助下，赴美留学并取得硕士学位，成为了美国公民。

商业巅峰与跌落

2000 年回国后，唐龙在上海崛起，（并迎娶了一位有着强大背景的漂亮女演员，事业蒸蒸日上。创立了一家成功的公司并将其上市。然而，他的商业帝国最终因管理不善而崩塌。他被卷入外汇诈骗案，被判刑 7 年，至今仍身处牢狱之中。他的公司股票暴跌，成为中国股市史上最大的失败案例之一。

3.4. 舒晓萍：梦中佳人

早年风采

舒晓萍，少女时代便拥有天姿聪慧，美貌绝伦。她是李飞初恋女友，也是陆程心中的暗恋对象。在中学时期，她的美貌和优异的学业成绩常常成为男孩子们争相追逐的对象，也因此常常引发男孩子间的争斗。

友情与爱情

大学期间，舒晓萍与李飞、唐龙关系密切，三人共同度过了青春时光，经历了各种喜怒哀乐。她差点陷入黑灯舞会的险境，幸亏李飞及时施以援手而脱险。毕业后，凭借优异的成绩被美国大学录取，与一位美国军官结婚并定居美国，成为可乐王公司的高级经理。

命运交汇

舒晓萍的丈夫在五角大楼工作，参与了许多中美之间的冲突事件。与此同时，她（他）与在中国国防部工作的陆程成为了工作关系上的朋友，尽管二人是对手，但在舒晓萍的影响下，他们建立了一种良好的合作关系。为中美关系的发展做出了贡献。

3.5. 杜雄：运动天才的沉沦

早年友情

杜雄是李飞的儿时玩伴，两人经常一起玩耍，也曾因打架而成为好朋友。他出生在贫困家庭，但拥有出色的运动天赋，尤其擅长短跑和足球。

命运转折

杜雄曾加入北京市少年足球队，然而由于性格上的不合，与教练发生了矛盾，最终被迫离开。此后，他的生活一蹶不振，多次因斗殴被公安拘留，甚至被判劳教。即便解除劳教后，他仍然过着浪荡不羁的生活，在街头摆摊为生，但性格上的暴烈导致他经常与人发生冲突。

友谊与绝望

李飞曾多次帮助杜雄，但命运却对他不利。杜雄再次因斗殴入狱，并逐渐染上了毒瘾。即便李飞尽力相助，但杜雄最终因为一次越狱行为被抓获，并在逃亡过程中不幸身亡，结束了一生的沉沦与绝望。

电影开场

【开场】北京，2017 年，白天，四合院内

【场景】

北京一座古色古香的四合院内，一台老式电话机静静地躺在桌子上。电话铃声突然响起，打破了室内的宁静。

李飞（背影）：

喂，我是李飞。什么？小学毕业四十五年同学聚会？

【场景快速切换】

上海外滩——一个女士（手持美国 XPhone 手机，极信语音）：收到，收到，一定参加！

广州——一个男人（华信手机，收到一条中华联通短信）：好的，我会准时到！

深圳——数字创新中心

一个年轻人在电脑上（QQ 小人头闪动，收到留言）：太棒了，终于可以见到老同学们了！

新西兰——一个家庭主妇（微窗电脑，收到一封海外邮件）：太好了，我一定会回去参加！

美国，亚特兰大——可乐王总部办公室

一个女高级主管（手腕上的苹果手表，收到 Facebook 留言）：好消息！我一定会参加！

所有画面定格，画外音响起：

画外音：通知五年级二班海内外同学，小学同学毕业四十五年后聚会将在北京香山举行。

李飞（背影，楠楠自语）：毕业都四十五年了，同学们都还好吗？

字幕开始："《时代梦》一部虚构的影片，取材于历史事件，但所有人物和情节均为虚构。"

【背景音乐】歌声：

东风吹，战鼓擂，

现在世界上究竟谁怕谁？

不是人民怕美帝，

而是美帝怕人民！

【字幕及独白】

1972 年，中国领袖毛泽东邀请美国总统尼克松访华，中美关系由此揭开了新的一页。

中国重返国际舞台，两位伟人用行动证明了他们的高瞻远瞩，对今天的世界政治格局产生了深远影响。

中美已成为世界上最具影响力的两个国家，他们将共同决定世界未来发展方向。

影片从 1972 年美国乒乓球队访华及随后的尼克松访华开始，通过五位同学的生活轨迹，将一个个重要历史事件串联展开。

主要事件

- 尼克松访华
- 文革后期
- 唐山地震
- 天安门事件
- 恢复高考
- 开放扫黄
- 八九学潮
- 南斯拉夫使馆被炸
- 中美撞机

- 香港回归
- 911
- 北京奥运
- 钓鱼岛
- 里巴巴美国上市
- 美国总统特朗普上台

2017 年，奥巴马下台，美国新总统特朗普上台，里巴巴市值跃身第一，中国 GDP 接近美国。

影片上部：1972 年至 1987 年，主要讲述 5 位同学李飞，陆程，唐龙，舒晓萍（女），杜雄从小学时代到大学的成长经历。

重点描述那个时代的特征，包括：

- 黄帅反潮流事件
- 基本物资配给匮乏
- 文革后期社会动荡
- 大院文化
- 街头流氓打架斗殴
- 少男少女恋爱
- 大学生活

【场景一】

岁月沉浸：1972 北京夜

【地点】北京，1972 年，夜晚，教室内

【画面】昏黄的灯光下，一间窄小的房间，陈设简单朴素。墙上挂着毛泽东画像和政治标语，散发着年代气息。

【声音】老式黑白电视机里传出嘈杂的声音，画面中是美国乒乓球队访华的场景。美国运动员们奇特的服装和发型引人注目。

【解说员（画外音）】1972 年，中美乒乓球友谊赛在北京举行。这是两国自 1949 年以来首次进行的重大体育交流活动，具有划时代的意义。

【人物】一位中年男子背对镜头坐在桌前，低声讲述着当时的社会背景。

【背景音乐】隐约传来《大海航行靠舵手》的歌声，与画面交织在一起，烘托出那个年代的特殊氛围。

【场景二】

小学政治课的烟云

【地点】北京，1972 年，夜晚（白天），住宅（学校）内

五年级二班的五位同学：李飞、陆程、龙宇、舒晓萍（女）、杜雄，是小学同班同学，从小一起玩耍。

这天，课堂上，同学们按照老师的要求背诵上级布置的尼克松访华政治口号。他们对美帝头子来中国访问感到困惑，纷纷向老师提出各种问题和建议：

"为什么邀请美帝访问？美帝是我们的敌人。"

"美国在我们脚下，一直挖下去就能到美国吗？"

"能不能抓起美帝头子开批斗会？"

"是否可以向尼克松高喊打倒美帝的口号……等等。"

老师面对同学们童言无忌的问题，有些哭笑不得。她反复强调，同学们必须按照上级领导的布置行事，不许有出格行为。如果有尼克松访华人员或外国记者问同学们问题，一定要按照上级统一部署背诵的内容回答。

同学们开始随着老师一起背诵:"美帝霸权,不得人心,越战失败,人民反战,内外交困,走投无路,来访我国……"

童声此起彼伏,课堂纪律开始混乱,嬉笑怒骂,天真烂漫。

【电影场景】

北京某小学,弥漫着浓厚的七十年代校园氛围。一位年轻漂亮的老师走进教室。

老师:同学们好,请起立,老师好。

老师在黑板上挂上了一幅地球仪。

老师:今天我们要上一堂特别的政治课。

她指着地球仪上的中国,说:

老师:同学们都知道,这是我们伟大的祖国,她的形状像一只雄鸡,老师喃喃自语,其实之前像个秋海棠叶子。

老师突然意识到有点失言,马上说:

老师:是雄鸡的形状,非常雄伟。

老师:今天想问同学们,你们知道美国吗?知道美国在地球的哪个位置吗?

知道的请举手回答。

老师开始点名：

李飞：美国是世界上最大的帝国主义国家，是我们的敌人。

陆程：美帝国主义侵略了朝鲜，我们抗美援朝打败了美帝野心狼。

龙宇：美帝占领了我们的宝岛台湾，帮助国民党蒋介石，阻挠我们解放台湾，统一祖国。

舒晓萍：我们打败了小日本，可是美帝继续扶植日本军国主义。

杜雄：美国有 3K 党，戴着黑面罩专门迫害黑人。

同学们开始高喊口号："打倒美帝国主义！美帝滚出台湾！"

老师：同学们都很有政治觉悟，说得非常好。

但今天老师要宣布一项重要事情，我们接到上级紧急通知，美国总统即将来中国访问。

同学们开始议论纷纷，一个同学大声问道：

同学 1：老师，为什么邀请美帝访问？美帝是我们的敌人。

另一个同学接口道：

同学 2：美国总统不就是美帝国主义的最大头子吗？怎么能让他来访问？

另一个同学插话道:

同学 3:听说美国在地球的下面,一直挖洞就能到美国。

大家开始议论纷纷:

同学 4:美帝国主义会不会真的挖洞打到中国来?

同学 5:美国总统怎么来中国啊?

老师:他们是乘飞机来的。

同学 6:那他一下飞机我们是不是就可以把他抓起来开批斗大会?

同学们哄堂大笑。

同学 7:我们要不要上街游行声讨美帝国主义?

同学们开始离开桌椅敲鼓(桌)跳舞,并高声唱道:

"东风吹,战鼓擂,现在世界上究竟谁怕谁?不是人民怕美帝,而是美帝怕人民。

得道多助,失道寡助,历史规律不可抗拒,美帝国主义必定灭亡,全世界人民一定胜利,全世界人民一定胜利!"

同学们情绪高涨,课堂纪律开始混乱。

老师大声说道:同学们请安静,根据上级的指示精神,同学们说的都不能做。我们还要欢迎美国总统访问中国，这是毛主席党中央英明决策。我们要听毛主席党中央的话，不容许有任何出格行为。

接下来，老师讲解了如何应对可能遇到的记者提问：

老师：如果有尼克松访华人员或外国记者问同学们问题，你们应该怎么回答呢？要按照上级的统一要求回答，每个同学都必须将背诵的内容牢记于心。

老师开始在黑板上写字，引导同学们一起朗读：

"美帝霸权，扰乱世界，不得人心，越战失败，走投无路，来访我国……"

童声此起彼伏。几个男女同学之间很亲密，交头接耳，弥漫着两小无猜的感觉。

【背景音乐】

（详细内容……见电影剧本）

这场戏突出了：

鲜明的七十年代学校背景；

教室布景灰暗但整洁；

老师点名同学名字；

老师年轻漂亮且知性；

同学们衣着朴素干净整齐，戴着红领巾；

讨论的话题严肃但又幽默好笑，体现了孩子们的天真无邪和口无遮拦；

几位同学特征明显，其中四男一女出众；

背诵的顺口溜完整，语言贴近时代。

【舞蹈重点】背景音乐响起，"东风吹，战鼓擂"，同学们开始跳舞并高唱。

【场景三】

街头红色风暴：1972 北京

【北京，1972 年，白天，街景】

【镜头】

摇镜头扫过 1972 年的北京街景，展现出川流不息的自行车洪流、昏暗的街道和灰色的建筑。

人群熙熙攘攘，面黄肌瘦但精神抖擞。他们穿着灰色的衣服，虽然朴素，却干净整洁，展现出鲜明的时代特征。

街道两旁挂满了标语，大喇叭里高声播放着批判意大利导演安东尼的电影《中国》的声音。

人群中不时响起革命口号，如"打倒苏修"、"打倒美帝"等。

【画外音】

（男声，低沉有力）

1972 年，正值文化大革命时期。中国大地笼罩在一片红色的海洋中。人们的思想和言行都受到严格的控制，任何与官方意识形态不符的东西都被视为异端。

【背景音乐】

（详细内容……见电影剧本）

【场景四】
尼克松访华下的百态人生

【夜，室外】

镜头缓缓扫过各个家庭：政府官员、机关干部、军队家庭、四合院、大杂院、平民区……无一不显示出极度的贫困。人们挤在一起，围着一个老旧的小黑白电视机，屏息凝神地观看。

【画面】

- 各家各户，人们端着饭碗，蹲在院子里，或是围坐在炉火旁，收听广播里传来的尼克松访华新闻报道。

- 电视画面反复播放着尼克松下飞机（与中国总理周恩来握手）的场景：他挥手致意，笑容满面。

- （人民大会堂）欢迎宴会上，乐队演奏着美国歌曲《美丽的美利坚》。

- 毛泽东主席与尼克松握手会谈。

【场景细节】

- 镜头捕捉到当时人们生活的缩影:

  有些家庭房间狭窄,大人小孩挤在一起睡觉,父母要极力避免让孩子看到尴尬的场面。

  警察上门查户口,要求成分不好分子在尼克松访华期间立即离开北京。

  人们用粮本、副食本、粮票等换取食物,生活物资匮乏。

- 一些人看着电视,发牢骚:"真可惜,这么好的茅台、烤鸭都款待帝国主义的头子了!"言语中充满了不满和不理解。

【画外音】

低沉的男声缓缓讲述着当时的历史背景……

【背景音乐】

《大海航行靠舵手干革命靠毛泽东思想》

《社会主义好共产党好

(详细内容……见电影剧本)

【场景五】
同学聚会

【**场景**】香山玉泉山脚下，一处豪华的四合院，傍晚时分。

【**时间**】2017 年

【人物】

- 五年级 2 班的四十位同学，年龄 55 岁左右
- 班主任老师
- 部分同学的儿女
- 一位美国同学的家人（通过视频）
- 一位同学的亲属

【场景描述】

镜头转回到 2017 年的北京，五年级 2 班的同学正在举行毕业四十五周年聚会。四十位同学，有的西装革履，有的穿着得体，有的穿着华丽，有的则身着休闲服装，从豪华汽车或步行中走出，相聚在香山玉泉山脚下的这处豪华四合院。

班主任老师在几位同学的陪伴下，站在门口迎接同学们到来。阔别多年，同学们见面分外激动，亲切地互相问候，回忆着往昔的校园趣事。

宴会厅内，装饰豪华，现代风格。背景大屏幕上播放着2017 年的新闻：习近平与马英九会面、里巴巴在美国纽约上市、中国 GDP 总量超过或接近美国等等。

主要同学寒暄见面后，电影的主要角色们走进宴会厅。他们虽然已年过半百，但依然精神抖擞，气质高雅。摄影师在现场拍照留念。

这场戏的重点是展现同学们的聚会场景。自助餐桌上摆满了各种精致菜肴，同学们举杯畅饮，谈笑风生。部分同学带着自己的儿女，为他们介绍昔日同窗。年轻人穿着时尚，青春靓丽，与父母辈的着装形成鲜明对比。他们玩着XPhone 手机，跳着拉丁舞，尽情享受着聚会的欢乐。

【特殊场景】

* 一位美国同学（家人）通过联邦快递送来大花篮鲜花，大屏幕上播放着他一家四口向北京的同学祝贺的视频。其中，丈夫是一位美国白人军官，上校军衔。
* 一位同学收到亲属寄来的信件，拆开后得知另一位同学已经去世，场面顿时变得凝重伤感。但很快，大家又恢复了正常，继续享受聚会。

- 一位残障人由漂亮的女儿推着轮椅出现，也加入了聚会的行列。

【舞蹈】

- 老派交谊舞
- 年轻人拉丁舞：Salsa、Bachata

【背景音乐】

"时光一去永不回，往事只能回味"

【人物对话】

人物对话应简洁明了，突出热烈的气氛。

【场景结束】

同学们在欢声笑语中度过了一个难忘的夜晚。

【场景六】

重温理想

【时间】1972 年

【地点】学校五年级二班

【人物】老师、学生

【场景描述】

镜头回到 1972 年的五年级二班，教室里一群衣着朴素的学生正热火朝天地讨论着。男生们围在一起，谈论着足球、篮球和哪个女生漂亮，谁可能和谁在谈恋爱；女生们则窃窃私语，神神秘秘地谈论着男女同学。偶尔有男同学过来招惹女生，引来一阵尖声的"臭流氓"，但也并没有真的生气，反而会应付几句。

一个男同学正兴致勃勃地扮演着样板戏智取威虎山中的滦平，学着他的腔调念道："天王盖地虎，宝塔镇河妖!"逗得同学们哈哈大笑。

这时，广播里传来一个熟悉的声音，是五年级二班的黄帅同学的事迹。广播里反复重复着："不学 ABC 我照样闹革命，学习不重要，学习毛泽东思想最重要。"

同学们议论纷纷，因为学校最近决定全部开卷考试，开展学工学农学军，还学习了张铁生白卷事件。

上课铃声响起，老师走进教室，开始语文理想课。少男少女们顿时收起玩心，开始眉目传情，相互递纸条。几个坏孩子则开始在课堂上捣乱，使得课堂纪律变得混乱。

今天老师讲的是如何树立正确的理想。对于长大后的理想，同学们纷纷踊跃发言。

多数同学表示长大后要当工人、农民、解放军，去打美帝苏修。

一个瘦瘦小小的男同学怯生生地说，他想有一个大房子，有很多房间，这样全家不用挤在一起睡觉。

他的话立刻招致了同学们的指责，说这是资产阶级臭思想，修正主义。同学们高喊口号："打到封、资、修臭思想！打到修正主义！"

老师不得不马上表态，说同学要有更远大的革命理想。要想到世界上还有三分之二的受苦大众生活在水深火热之中，美国黑人正在遭受苦难，台湾还没有回归伟大祖国怀抱，都需要我们去解放。同学们不能只停留在农民的思想"30 亩地一头牛，老婆孩子热炕头"。

一个女同学说，爸爸告诉她参考消息刊登文章说美国人发明了一种机器，叫做水果电脑，能模仿人的脑子思考，还能写东西。

她的话音刚落，就遭到了同学们的起哄，说她是崇洋媚外的思想。一个男孩从女孩书包里偷拿出一个苹果，咬了一口扔回给女孩，说："是用这个思考吗？"

众同学哄堂大笑，女孩看着被咬了一口的苹果，趴在桌子上哭了起来。（一个苹果被咬下一口的特写镜头）

另一个女孩说长大后希望能周游世界，立刻遭到同学们的指责："你是不是想投敌叛国啊？"

女孩们顿时吓得不敢说话。

一个男孩子看不下去，出面袒护女孩，却遭致几个坏孩子的不满。他们突然开始打斗，高喊反潮流口号，称今后谁的拳头厉害谁就能闹革命。

【背景音乐】

【场景分析】

这一场景展现了 1972 年特殊年代下，五年级二班学生们对于理想的不同理解和追求。他们对未来充满憧憬，却又受到当时社会环境的限制。

【场景七】

室外 / 运动场

【时间】下午课间

（下课铃声响起，学生们像一群快乐的小鸟，从教室里飞奔出来，涌向运动场。）

男孩们像脱了缰的野马，活力四射。他们有的在操场上挥舞着棒球，尽情地打着球；有的在篮球场上你追我赶，激烈地比赛；还有的在足球场上奋力拼搏，展现着矫健的身姿；乒乓球台上，乒乓球上下翻飞，发出清脆的声响，引得围观者阵阵喝彩。

女孩们则聚集在另一边，为即将到来的学校庆祝活动做准备。她们身着鲜艳的服装，脸上洋溢着青春的笑容。有的三五成群，低声地讨论着舞蹈动作；有的在音乐老师的指导下，认真地练习着歌声；还有的在舞台上排练着舞蹈，优美的舞姿仿佛盛开的鲜花。

整个运动场充满了欢声笑语，热闹非凡。

【重点】

- 运动：通过描写男孩子们打棒球、篮球、足球、乒乓球等运动，展现学生们活泼、健康的形象。

- 编舞：着重描写女孩们排练舞蹈的场景，展现她们的青春活力和艺术气息。

- 音乐：通过音乐老师的指导和女孩们的歌声，烘托欢快、积极的氛围。

【场景八】
防空演习变演练

【时间】 夜晚

【地点】 室内

一天的繁忙生活即将结束，孩子们向毛泽东塑像行了一礼后，躺在床上准备入睡。

午夜，突然传来急促的防空警报声，吵醒了他们。有人高声呼喊，是美帝飞机来犯，赶快进入防空洞。

大家慌乱地穿好衣服，匆忙下楼躲进地下室。

与此同时，邻里间开始秩序井然地转移孩子们。大家有条不紊地走向防空洞，安全地躲避可能的威胁。

然而，随后的喇叭声宣布这只是一次防空演习。有些孩子发现自己穿反了裤子，引来了大家的欢笑。

接着，大喇叭响起领袖又发表了"最高指示"的声音响彻街头，"千万不要忘记阶级斗争"。孩子们异常兴奋，开始在街上举行彩旗游行，一片热闹景象。

男女学生在学校举行的游行中相遇，偷偷牵起了手。

大街上，几个人被戴着高帽五花大绑捆着游行过来，人群中高喊"他们是美帝间谍，收听美国之音广播"，众人向他们身上睡吐沫、扔香蕉皮、鸡蛋皮；被带走参加批斗。场面让人感到心酸。

男子低沉的画外音叙述着当时的社会背景，批斗会的场面迅速闪现。

【重点】背景音乐

【场景九】
2016 年同学聚会

【**时间**】2016 年

【**地点**】香山

【**场景**】室内外豪华宴会

镜头转回 2016 年的同学聚会，豪华现代的宴会场景与 1972 年的简朴画面形成强烈反差。

同学们相互敬酒，谈笑风生，气氛热烈。这时，电视新闻吸引了大家的注意。

一位里巴巴的高层，青云，开始讲述在美国上市如何筹措到至今为止的最大资金，如何受美国人民追捧。电视上出现了奥巴马洋洋得意的笑脸，以及美国大选特朗普与希拉里辩论的激烈场面。

随后，画面切换到台湾马英九与习近平在新加坡会见的画面，以及中国航空母舰、钓鱼岛局势等新闻。

宴会继续进行，场面依然豪华、温暖、热情。男主角邀请女主角跳舞，两人目光对视，含情脉脉，陷入沉默，开始回忆过去的美好时光。

【**背景音乐**】舒缓浪漫的音乐

【**细节描写**】

宴会场景可以更加具体地描写，例如：宾客们身着华丽的服装，觥筹交错，谈笑风生。

青云讲述在美国上市的经历时，可以加入一些具体的细节，例如：他如何克服困难，如何赢得投资人的信任等等。

电视新闻画面可以剪辑得更加紧凑，以增强戏剧效果。

男主角和女主角跳舞时，可以加入一些肢体语言和表情描写，以展现两人的情感变化。

【场景十】
义愤填膺

【时间】 1976 年

【地点】 北京市某中学校门口

画面切换至中学门口。学生们成群结队地走出校门，亲切地交谈着，笑容洋溢。他们已经长大了，女孩们亭亭玉立，青春靓丽。

一些人群聚集在校门口，他们正在交谈着，有的抽着烟，有的吹着口哨。突然，他们注意到了一个瘦弱的女学生，名叫舒晓萍。几个学生走向舒晓萍，开始打量着她。

舒晓萍感到有些不安，试图摆脱，但无济于事。就在这时，李飞、陆程和杜雄看到了情况，他们立即走上前去，帮助舒晓萍摆脱困境。

李飞和陆程以和平方式，劝说学生们离开。杜雄则从地上拾起一块石头，但并未使用。学生们逐渐明白了情况，最终离开了。

在其他同学的帮助下，李飞成功地将舒晓萍带出了人群。他们逃脱了潜在的危险，但仍然感到心有余悸。

【背景音乐】 激昂、紧张

【场景十一】
室外 / 夜 / 公园

【场景描述】

夜幕降临，公园里静悄悄的，只有昏黄的路灯闪烁着微光。树影婆娑，花香四溢，空气中弥漫着一种浪漫的气息。男主角和女主角漫步在林荫小道上，两人的身影被拉得长长的。男主角英俊帅气，女主角美丽动人，他们低声交谈着，脸上洋溢着幸福的笑容。

【人物动作】

男主角突然停下了脚步，转过身，深情地看着女主角。女主角也停下了脚步，两人的目光相遇，彼此眼中都充满了爱意。

【人物台词】

男主角：（深情地）我爱你，晓萍。

女主角：（感动地）我也爱你，飞。

男主角：（想要拥吻女主角）

【场景变化】

突然，几个手持大棒的工人民兵从黑暗中冲了出来，将两人团团围住。

【人物动作】

工人民兵：（大声地）你们两个在干什么？

男主角：（惊讶地）我们在约会。

工人民兵：（怒斥道）谈恋爱？这里是公园，不是你们谈情说爱的地方！

【场景变化】

工人民兵粗暴地将男主角和女主角推搡着，带到了工宣队。

【场景结束】

【场景十二】
室内 / 工宣队驻地

审讯现场气氛紧张，灯光昏暗，充满了压抑的气氛。

画外音： 在那段黑暗的日子里，工宣队驻地的审讯常常在深夜进行，人们的命运在这里被决定。一位年轻的女孩，被她的家长接回家，脸上写满了复杂的情绪。

【场景十三】
室外 / 大街上

李飞独自回家，突然遭到袭击，他受伤严重，但艰难地（爬）回到家中；得知李飞受伤，有同学立即通知了舒晓萍。尽管面对家长的反对，舒晓萍毅然出门，冲向李飞所在的地方；

舒晓萍搀扶着李飞回到家中，她焦急地为他处理伤口。两人紧紧相拥，表达彼此的关爱和担忧。他们亲吻着，共同面对未来的挑战。

【场景十四（1）】

室外 / 大街上

李飞和杜雄联络了一群人，准备报复。画面切换至大院门口，两群人（手持器械，）互相对峙，情绪激动（打斗一触即发）。突然，一名人员试图冲过去，引起混乱，但很快被其他人制止了。人群中有不同服装的人，代表着不同的社会群体，画面切换至，（双方怒目相对）的场景，有人在分发（永恒牌香烟），（表达他们的诉求和意见，而不是分发武器。人们聚集在一起，共同讨论，没有出现分发武器的场景。删去）警察乘坐车辆出现，制止了混乱局面，但没有发生激烈的冲突。背景音乐营造了紧张的气氛，但没有加剧暴力情绪。

【时代典型特征】

李飞，杜雄联系众人开始报复，场面紧张；

【镜头】

大院门口两群人手持器械相互对垒；

打架开始升级，演发群架；

约架场面，各个大院整齐的划一的不同服装，

海军，陆军，空军，机关大院，居民区各不一样，

羊圈容帽子，军跨，白口罩，

聚集团伙分发香烟的场景，根据不同的群体划分。

场面壮观火药味十足。冲突千钧一发之际，

乘坐吉普，摩托，自行车的警察突然出现，

人群大乱，四散奔逃。

【背景音乐】

【场景十四（2）】
室外 / 大街上

【地点】室内 / 派出所

【人物】

- 李飞：男主角，少年
- 舒晓萍：女主角，少女
- 警察：两名，中年男性

【场景描述】

李飞和舒晓萍被带到派出所，两名警察正在对他们进行询问。

警察1（用方言）："你们在公园里做什么？解释清楚。"

李飞和舒晓萍紧握着彼此的手，眼神坚定，不愿详细描述私事。

李飞："我们没有做任何违法的事。"

舒晓萍："我们是清白的。"

警察见他们如此强硬，也无法奈何，只好放他们离开了。

李飞（走出派出所门口，拉住舒晓萍的手）："谢谢你！"

舒晓萍："我们一起面对，没有什么可怕的。"

李飞："我们不会屈服于不公正的对待。"

【画外音】同学杜雄被判三年劳教。

男子低沉画外音："那时的社会动荡，公审大会的场面闪过。"

【画面】街道上，高音大喇叭播放着评论意大利摄影师拍摄的影片《中国》。

【画外音】社会动乱，思想混乱，物质匮乏，人们在等待着巨变。

【背景音乐】悲伤、压抑的音乐

【画面】街头巷尾，各种顺口溜、小曲在人们口口相传。
顺口溜：刀子板带，腰里腰外，飞轮匕首，哥们儿全有，要茬架，东单西四鼓楼前，北海后门颐和园…

画外音：在那个动荡不安的年代，人们用自己的方式表达着对生活的抗争和对未来的期盼。

【场景结束】

【场景十五】
黎明破晓，地震突袭

【场景】 室内外

【时间】 黎明

【音效】 宁静的鸟鸣，逐渐被远处隐约的轰鸣声取代

【画面】

- 一缕缕阳光穿过窗帘，照亮了简朴的房间。
- 屋内，一家三口正围坐在餐桌旁，享用着简单的早餐。
- 父亲脸上洋溢着幸福的笑容，母亲温柔地为孩子盛粥，孩子则天真地玩弄着手中的玩具。
- 窗外，鸟儿欢快地歌唱，花草在微风中轻轻摇曳，一切都是那么平静祥和。

【画外音】 1976 年 7 月 28 日，唐山，一个普通的黎明。

【音效】 轰鸣声越来越近，越来越强烈，仿佛来自地狱的怒吼。

【画面】

- 突然，画面开始剧烈地摇晃，房屋发出嘎吱嘎吱的声响，桌椅板凳东倒西歪。
- 一家三口惊恐地站起身，还没来得及反应，天花板便轰然倒塌，碎石瓦砾铺天盖地而来。
- screams 划破了宁静的早晨，一切都陷入了一片混乱和黑暗。

【背景音乐】 紧张、急促的音乐，突显地震的突然和猛烈

【场景十六】

天安门广场，朗诵声震人心

【**场景**】室外，天安门广场

【**时间**】白天

【**画面**】

- 天安门广场上，人山人海，黑压压的人群汇成了一片红色的海洋。
- 毛泽东主席的巨幅画像悬挂在天安门城楼上，神情庄严。
- 人群中，一位青年站在纪念碑前，高举着毛主席语录，声音洪亮地朗诵着："欲哭闻鬼叫，我哭豺狼笑，祭泪洒英杰，扬眉剑出鞘！"

【**音效**】慷慨激昂的朗诵声，回荡在广场上空。

【**画面**】黑夜，人群突然骚动，四周出现了大量工人民兵，从天安门、人民大会堂、历史博物馆、前门大街四个方向包围过来。画面转向黑压压的工人民兵，手持大棒，冲向人群。邓小平成为替罪羊再次被打倒。

【画外音】1976 年 9 月 9 日，毛泽东主席逝世，举国哀悼。与此同时，四人帮被粉碎，中国迎来了新的历史转折。

【背景音乐】悲壮、激昂的音乐，交织着时代的悲痛和希望

【场景十七】
别离与新生

【场景】 室外 / 劳教所 / 大学

【画面】 少年少女们含着泪水，依依惜别。他们刚刚探望了在劳教所的同学杜雄，心中感慨万千。告别之后，他们各奔东西，迈入了大学的校门。

【画面切换】 各大学，军校同学入校的画面，镜头闪过各所大学、军校，新生们报到、入学的场景。他们脸上洋溢着青春的活力，对未来充满了憧憬。

【背景音乐】 激昂的音乐声渐渐隐去，取而代之的是舒缓的旋律，仿佛诉说着时代的变迁。

【画外音】 在告别的泪水中，他们踏上了新的征程，每个人心中都怀揣着希望与梦想。时代在变迁，他们也在成长。

【场景十八】

社会巨变

影片开始描述 1977 年至 1986 年大学状况和中国社会状况

1977 年至 1986 年，中国经历了巨大的社会变革。大学招生制度改革，恢复高考，使得大批青年学生重返校园，为国家发展注入了新的活力。与此同时，中国对外开放的大门逐渐打开，西方文化和思想开始涌入，冲击着传统的社会观念。

【画面切换】

画面展示了校园里充满活力的学生们，他们在课堂上认真听讲，在操场上挥洒汗水。画外音解释着这一时期的教育改革和社会变迁。

【室内 / 家庭 / 夜】

夜晚，万家灯火。各个家庭的黑白电视机正播放着日本电影，展示日本繁华的街道和华丽的服装，令观众们感到新奇和震撼。

【音效】

日本电影的主题曲悠扬地回荡在房间里，营造出一种新奇和略带不安的氛围。

【画面切换】

电视机屏幕上，美国电影的激烈枪战场面将观众带入另一个世界。主人公的英勇无畏让许多年轻人热血沸腾。

【背景音乐】

紧接着，电影中的音乐变化为舒缓的旋律，配合着电视画面中展示的西方文化。

【画面切换】

电影中的某些场景让家长们感到不安，他们纷纷关掉电视，将孩子赶去睡觉。

【音效】

家庭里的录音机播放着港台流行歌曲，邓丽君的《何日君再来》和《小城故事多》。

【画外音】

世界的大门已经打开，关不住了。这一夜，许多人辗转难眠。他们无法再将自己封闭在狭小的世界里，外面的世界已经打开了大门，他们迫切地想要去探索，去感受。

【背景音乐】

舒缓的旋律继续，画面逐渐暗淡，展现出对未来的无限憧憬。

【场景十九】

大学舞会

【室内 / 宿舍 / 大学】

【时间】 傍晚

【人物】

- 女主角：舒晓萍，中文系学生，活泼开朗，对新鲜事物充满好奇。
- 闺蜜：王小美，英语系学生，时尚前卫，敢于挑战传统。
- 男同学1号：李飞，建筑系学生，阳光帅气，热爱运动。
- 男同学2号：唐龙，经济系学生，幽默风趣，才华横溢。

【场景描述】

随着音乐的节奏，大学舞会里，年轻的学生们尽情释放着青春的活力。舒晓萍和王小美身着色彩鲜艳的衣裙，与李飞和唐龙翩翩起舞。他们脸上洋溢着幸福的笑容，沉浸在欢乐的氛围中。

宿舍里，几个同学围坐在电视机前，观看新闻节目。画面中，1979 年对越战争的硝烟弥漫，1981 年美国总统遇刺的震惊世界，1982 年马拉多纳的辉煌时刻，1984 年马岛战争的剑拔弩张，都一一闪过。

与此同时，各种广告也出现在电视上，广告词朗朗上口，展示着田中汽车、汉堡镇和可乐王的品牌标志，展现了资本主义生活方式的冲击。

突然，电视画面切换到 1984 年洛杉矶奥运会的消息，中国选手许先生夺得男子自选手枪慢射金牌，这是中国奥运会历史上第一枚金牌！同学们顿时沸腾起来，他们欢呼雀跃，用各种方式庆祝这一历史性的时刻。

【背景音乐】

迪斯科舞曲和时代金曲交替播放，营造出欢快而充满活力的氛围。

【场景二十】
逃学去深圳

【室外 / 广州 /1984 年】

【时间】 白天

【人物】

男主角 1 号：李飞，高中毕业进入 xx 大学后开始厌学，与有同样想法的同学男 3 号，唐龙，请假逃学去深圳倒卖电子表、T 恤等用品准备回北京贩卖。

【场景描述】

李飞和唐龙站在广州火车站的站台上，他们准备搭乘火车前往深圳。他们眼神中充满了期待和兴奋，这是他们第一次逃学，也是他们第一次去南方。

火车一路向南，窗外风景飞速掠过。李飞和唐龙望着窗外的景色，心中思绪万千。他们憧憬着深圳的繁华，也梦想着用自己的双手创造财富。

终于，火车抵达了深圳。李飞和唐龙下了火车，眼前的高楼大厦让他们目瞪口呆。他们深吸一口气，迈着矫健的步伐，向这个充满机遇的城市进发。

【场景画面】

深圳罗湖边境中英一条街的画面

街道上人头攒动，各种商品琳琅满目

李飞和唐龙穿梭在人群中，寻找商机

【背景音乐】

80 年代流行音乐，粤语歌曲

【场景二十一】
困境之路：拘留所的艰辛

【室内 / 拘留所 / 深圳】

李飞发现唐龙留下的字条，得知他失踪了。焦急万分的李飞立即报警求助。经过一番调查，李飞终于得知了唐龙的下落：他被当地人诱惑，试图偷渡香港转道美国，结果被香港警察截获并遣送回国，现被公安机关羁押。

李飞心急如焚，赶到拘留所探望唐龙。然而，眼前的景象让他震惊：拘留所的环境让人感到无助。

【镜头】

拘留所。拥挤的房间里，许多人挤在一起，空气混浊。李飞看到唐龙，目光中充满了焦虑和疲惫。

李飞看着这一切，心里充满了无力感。他试图向看守所求情，但最终却无功而返。

【背景音乐】

悲伤的音乐声中，李飞只能独自一人返回北京。

【场景二十二】

光荣与梦想：国强电器的奋斗岁月

【室外 / 出国人员服务部 / 北京】

回到学校后，李飞依然利用课余时间在出国人员服务部门前倒卖电器赚取外快。在这里，他结识了同样来自广东的黄氏两兄弟。众人经常在一起交流，倒卖电器、谈天说地。然而，由于学业等因素，李飞最终没能继续这项生意。

【画外音】

那个年代，经贸部有很多人公派出国。国家规定，长期出国人员可以购买一些电器，一年限额为 4 大 8 小。有些家庭用不了这些电器，就转卖给了像李飞这样的倒卖者。这群人起初主要是北京本地人，后来逐渐有了更多外地人的加入，其中以广东人为主。他们是当时中国进口电器贸易的开创者之一，也是这个时代的一大特点。

【室外 / 阜成门外甲 1 号 / 北京】

广东的朋友们总是围着李飞，用方言交谈，有时候李飞会感到不耐烦，但他也知道这是彼此之间的交流障碍。不过，黄氏两兄弟的态度却是异常谦和，他们每天都会给所有的电器倒卖者发烟，显示了他们的善意和友好。

【镜头】

成立《国强电器》

画面上，黄氏兄弟站在国强电器的门前，笑容满面。他们从当初在街头巷尾倒卖电器的小商贩，成长为中国家电零售业的领军企业之一。他们的故事，也成为了中国改革开放时代的一个缩影。

【场景二十三】
迷失的青春

【地点】 室内 / 舞会 / 北京

【人物】

- 唐龙：男主角，被释放后隐瞒情况回校继续上学
- 李飞：男二号，唐龙的同学
- 舒晓萍：女主角，唐龙与李飞的小学同学
- 女同学：唐龙邀请参加舞会的女生

【场景描述】

灯光昏暗的舞会现场，音乐声震耳欲聋，一对对男女在暧昧的灯光下狂舞。唐龙、李飞、舒晓萍和另一个女同学也融入了这场纸醉金迷的狂欢中。

唐龙自暴自弃，沉迷于这种糜烂的生活，甚至频繁出入私人举办的"黑灯舞会"。他邀请李飞和舒晓萍参加，但他们并不知道这其中的风险。

今晚，他们参加了一场私人舞会。四位同学在舞池中尽情释放着心中的压抑，却逐渐产生了争执。李飞和舒晓萍想

要离开，唐龙却坚持留下，另一个女同学则犹豫不决。

突然，公用电话响起，舒晓萍接到远方军校陆程打来的电话。她情绪激动，声音哽咽。

就在这时，舞会灯光突然熄灭，传来男女的尖叫声，场面顿时陷入混乱。

关键时刻，李飞为了保护舒晓萍，挥拳打倒几个扑向她的男人，拉着她逃出舞场。而唐龙和另一个女生则被卷入混乱中，有人举报，警察突至，唐龙被抓。

【重点】

【舞蹈】（根据具体场景选择合适的舞蹈类型）

【背景音乐】 动感十足的舞曲，节奏感强，营造狂欢的氛围

【场景二十四】
审 判

【地点】 室内 / 法庭

【人物】

- 法官
- 唐龙
- 律师
- 旁听席上的李飞和舒晓萍

【场景描述】

镜头转至法庭，法官宣布了判决结果：唐龙因涉嫌参与非法聚会，被判处了半年的监禁，并受到了学校的开除处分。

旁听席上的李飞和舒晓萍目睹了唐龙的判决，心中充满了悲伤和感慨。曾经一起度过的美好时光，如今却被现实的审判所打破，让他们感到十分心痛。

【场景二十五】
军校的思念

【地点】桂林军校，室外

【人物】

- 男 2 号（陆程）：军校学员，接到舒晓萍的来信，得知唐龙入狱的情况。一直暗恋舒晓萍，但默默埋藏在内心，与李飞是铁哥们。
- 舒晓萍：陆程暗恋的对象，发来书信告知他唐龙的情况。

【场景描述】

陆程在桂林军校的训练场上，严肃地进行着军事训练。阳光透过树梢，洒在他挺拔的身姿上，映衬出一股坚毅的气质。突然，一名战友递来一封信，是舒晓萍的来信。陆程心中一动，急忙拆开，得知了唐龙入狱的消息。他的眉头紧锁，心中涌起一股难以言喻的痛楚。

在忙碌的训练间隙，陆程偷偷拿出舒晓萍的来信，仔细阅读。信中的每一个字都仿佛是她亲口对他说的，令他的心情异常澎湃。然而，他深知自己与舒晓萍之间的距离，只能将心中的思念深深埋藏，不让她知道，为了减轻内心的情感纠葛，他决定更加努力地投入军队的训练。

【剧情发展】

- 阅兵仪式的壮观场面，展现出军校学员的飒爽英姿。
- 军队训练的严苛环境，展现出陆程坚韧不拔的品格和军人的铁骨柔情。

【背景音乐】

悠扬的军乐声渐起，交织在场景中，彰显出军人的豪情壮志。

【场景二十六】
逆境之路：从出狱到足球场

【外景 / 北京】

【时间】八十年代末

【场景】

1. 出狱

杜雄，男，20 岁出头，身形瘦削，眼神带着一丝狠厉。他拖着沉重的步伐走出监狱的大门，深吸了一口自由的空气，却感到迷茫和无助。

2. 西瓜摊

杜雄来到一个街角，摆了一个西瓜摊。他卖力地吆喝着，但生意并不景气。他看着来来往往的人群，心中充满了愤懑。

3. 踢球

李飞，男，20 岁出头，大学在读，酷爱足球。他看到杜雄，便走过来招呼他一起踢球。杜雄犹豫了一下，最终还是答应了。

【场景切换】

出狱、西瓜摊、踢球的画面快速闪过

【背景音乐】

激昂的音乐声渐起，与画面交织在一起，展现出杜雄内心的挣扎与渴望。

【旁白】

时间进入八十年代末，同学大学毕业后各奔东西，杜雄却因为打架斗殴而锒铛入狱。出狱后，他无业可依，只能靠摆西瓜摊维持生计。李飞不忍看他自暴自弃，经常招呼他去参加足球比赛。在足球场上，杜雄找到了久违的快乐和自信，也逐渐开始反省自己过去的行为。

【场景结束】

《时代梦》第一部　完

《时代梦》第二部

　　李飞大学毕业后进入国企工作，后被派驻香港。九十年代初，他开始在广东和海南经营大宗商品进口业务。这段经历让他亲身见证了 1997 年香港回归，以及当时疯狂的进口商品走私活动。他还结识了多年后在国内外赫赫有名的走私人物赖氏团伙成员，并险些丧命于黑社会及腐败公检法手中。

　　生意过程中的危险遭遇，以及国企复杂的人际关系，使李飞感到极度失望，萌生了去意。他选择移民国外，并对国外良好的生活工作环境留下了深刻印象。然而，在国外，他也感到失落迷茫。最终，他于 2005 年返回国内，重新创业。

【场景二十七】

触摸改革的脉搏：广州出口交易会

【地点】 室外，广州 / 深圳

【时间】 白天

【人物】 李飞

【剧情】

李飞第一次乘飞机参加广州出口交易会，会场内人头攒动，热闹非凡。各式各样的商品琳琅满目，来自世界各地的客商摩肩接踵，讨价还价。李飞目不暇接，感受着改革开放的浪潮滚滚而来。李飞目睹了深圳股票交易开幕，交易所人群熙熙攘攘，人们涌向柜台进行股票交易，李飞感到一片陌生。

【场景二十八】

封闭的友谊：北京友谊商店事件

【地点】 室内外，友谊商店，北京

【时间】 白天

【人物】 李飞，门卫

【剧情】

李飞从广州回到北京，听说北京友谊商店可以买到进口商品，便兴冲冲地赶了过去。然而，当他来到门口时，却被门卫拦住，告知只有外国人才能进入。

李飞顿时怒火中烧，指着门卫大声斥责道："你以为这里是上海英法租界吗？凭什么中国人不能进去？！"说完，他便推开门卫，冲进了商店。

店内的工作人员见状，立刻上前阻止李飞，并报警将他带到了派出所。经过一番解释和教育，李飞最终被释放。

【场景二十九】

别离与命运：舒晓萍的异国情缘

【室内 / 首都机场】

李飞赶到机场，与陆程一起送别舒晓萍。唐龙即将前往美国留学。

机场广播：

"搭乘 XX 班机去美国纽约的旅客请登机。"

泪别

舒晓萍与唐龙依依惜别，与陆程挥手告别。

【背景音乐】

音乐声起，镜头切换到美国。

【美国】

舒晓萍和唐龙开始了他们的海外留学生活。

【纽约曼哈顿】

镜头闪过纽约曼哈顿岛的双世贸中心。

背景音乐响起：（换成自有版权的音乐）

【校园咖啡厅】

舒晓萍在学校咖啡厅与一位美国军官相识，并坠入爱河结婚。这位美国军官在五角大楼工作。

【舒晓萍的魅力】

舒晓萍从小就是学校明星，聪明漂亮，一直是男孩追逐的对象。在大学期间，她更是舞会明星，差点卷入黑灯舞会。

【命运的交错】

舒晓萍嫁给的美国军官，因工作原因，与后来同是在中国军队国防部工作的陆程建立了良好的工作关系。他们既有合作，又有交锋，但开始彼此都并不知道，这位美国军官竟是娶了过去的暗恋情人。

【场景三十】
辩论朝鲜战争：中美关系的纷争

【地点】美国大学教室

【时间】1987 年

【人物】

- 教授
- 美国学生
- 舒晓萍
- 美国军官

【场景描述】

教授：同学们，今天我们来讨论一个非常重要的话题，那就是韩国战争对中美关系的影响。

美国学生 1：我认为是北韩首先发起了战争，美国是依据联合国决议出兵干预的。

美国学生 2：我同意，美国的行为是为了捍卫民主。

舒晓萍：我有不同的看法。我认为朝鲜战争是一场复杂的冲突，涉及多个利益和影响因素。美国的介入确实阻止了共产主义在朝鲜的扩张，但也给朝鲜半岛带来了长期的分裂和动荡。

美国学生 3：你这是在为北韩的侵略行为辩护！

舒晓萍：我并不是在为北朝鲜辩护，而是认为我们需要客观看待历史，理解各方的立场和动机。

美国军官：我想分享一些看法。我认为韩战是中美关系恶化的重要因素。战争造成了双方巨大的伤亡和痛苦，中国领导人毛甚至失去了自己的儿子，这为未来的对立埋下了伏笔。

美国军官：战争结束后，中国对国内民族资本家进行了清算，没收了他们的财产。美国开始对中国实施全面经济封锁，导致中国全面闭关锁国，与世隔绝。

舒晓萍：(对军官产生好感，感激的望着他)

【场景结束】

【场景三十一】

意外邂逅：爱与和平的交汇

【地点】咖啡厅

【时间】1987 年

【人物】

- 舒晓萍
- 美国军官

【场景描述】

舒晓萍和美国军官在咖啡厅意外邂逅。

美国军官：舒晓萍小姐，你好。

舒晓萍：你好。

美国军官：今天在课堂上，我对我的美国同学的言论向你道歉。

舒晓萍：没关系，我能理解他们的想法。

美国军官：我很高兴能遇到你。你是一个很有见地的人。

舒晓萍：谢谢你。

两人开始交谈，发现彼此有很多共同话题。

咖啡厅背景电视正在播放：美国航天飞机爆炸，苏联切尔诺贝利核泄漏。

舒晓萍：世界真是太不安宁了。

美国军官：是啊，我们应该一起努力，为世界和平做贡献。

两人相识，开始约会。

【场景结束】

【背景音乐】 舒缓的钢琴曲

【场景三十二（1）】
天安门广场的挑战

【地点】

镜头切换至北京，天安门，1989 年 6 月 4 日凌晨。

【场景描述】

天安门广场上聚集了大量的抗议者，他们手举标语，高喊口号，场面紧张而激动人心。

镜头再次转向北京木樨地街口。

李飞牵着女友的手，焦急地注视着西面。一大队军车呼啸而过，车上的士兵紧张而警惕，仿佛随时准备应对任何情况。

军车队经过时，人群中有人试图阻止它们前进，但很快被警察制止了。

突然，局势失控，有人开始向军车投掷石块，警察不得不采取行动，局面陷入混乱。

镜头切换至天安门广场。

抗议者与警察爆发了冲突，嘈杂的声音充斥着整个广场。警察试图驱散人群，抗议者则不愿离开，坚定地表达自己的诉求。

镜头再次转向美国。

【场景结束】

【场景三十二（2）】
婚礼与人权

【地点】 室内 / 婚礼现场 /1989/ 美国

【镜头】 在美国，舒晓萍的婚礼现场。舒晓萍与她的美国军官丈夫在门口迎接客人，唐龙带着他的漂亮女友到场。在宴会上，客人们享受着美好的时光。

突然间，电视转播中出现了一场中国的政治活动画面，引起了来宾们的一些讨论。一些客人表达了关注和担忧。

舒晓萍、她的军官丈夫和其他客人发生了争执。她试图捍卫国家的尊严。

美国电视转播中，国际领导人对中国政府的行为表示担忧，呼吁尊重人权和民主价值观。

婚礼继续进行，来宾们继续享受着这个特殊的时刻。舒晓萍感到一些内心的矛盾和不安，但她努力保持微笑，不让自己的情绪影响婚礼的气氛。

晚会结束后，舒晓萍和她的丈夫回到了房间。他们坐在一起，静静地聊着彼此的感受和想法。他们尊重对方的立场，试图理解彼此的观点。

【场景三十二（3）】

倾诉与拥抱：北京的黑夜与情感释放

【画面再度回到北京】

夜幕降临，李飞与女友站在家中的凉台上，注视着远处的街道，灯光昏暗，而军车车队的灯光在远处闪烁。高音喇叭声远远传来，播放着戒严通告，街道上人来人往，但是在大学附近却显得寂静。

收音机里传来了一篇社论："中国政府镇压和平抗议者的行为已经引起了全球的谴责，这一行径将对中美关系产生深远的影响。"

两人心情沉重，他们表达了内心的悲伤和愤怒，但没有采取极端的方式。他们互相搂抱，试图给对方一些安慰。

【画面切换】 柏林墙倒塌，苏联独联体国家解体。

【重点】 街道上人们匆匆忙忙的身影、远处军车的灯光闪烁、收音机里播放的社论声，以及两人之间的情感交流。

【背景音乐逐渐响起】

【场景三十三】
告别与决定

【地点】室内 / 家庭 / 美国

【人物】

- 舒晓萍
- 舒晓萍的先生
- 唐龙

【场景描述】

舒晓萍夫妻和唐龙围坐在客厅，准备送别唐龙回中国。电视里播放着海湾战争的报道，同时插播了邓小平南巡讲话的片段。

【对话】

舒晓萍：唐龙，你真的决定要回中国吗？我知道中国正在进行改革开放，但你在美国已经有了一份不错的生活。

唐龙：是的，我已经决定回国了。我觉得我可以在中国的发展中发挥更大的作用。

舒晓萍的丈夫：但是中国的环境和制度与美国有很大的不同，你需要做好适应的准备。

唐龙：我明白。我会尽力去适应并努力工作。

【背景音乐】

【场景三十四】
夜幕之前的忧虑

【地点】室外 / 香港街景 /1997 年

【场景描述】

镜头闪过香港维多利亚港的夜景，灯火辉煌，璀璨夺目。唐龙返回中国，在香港与李飞会面。

此时的香港正处于 1997 年回归中国的前夕，人心惶惶，弥漫着忧虑的气氛。

李飞与唐龙开车在香港大道上一路目睹香港的繁华夜景，高楼大厦与繁忙的交通，但也能够感受到回归前的政治和经济不确定性。

【对话】

李飞：唐，你终于回来了！

唐龙：是啊，我回来了！

李飞：现在香港的情况很复杂，你要小心一点。

唐龙：我知道。我会注意的。

【香港背景音乐】

《蓝莲花》《相思小蚂蚁》

【场景三十五】
香港回归前的交汇

【地点】香港兰桂坊酒吧

【时间】1997 年

【人物】唐龙、李飞

【场景描述】

兰桂坊酒吧街，霓虹灯闪烁，熙熙攘攘的人影。唐龙和李飞坐在吧台边，两人低声交谈着。

【对话】

唐龙：我决定去上海发展。

李飞：上海？那边机会很多，不过你要小心行事。

唐龙：放心吧，我会小心的。

从酒吧的电视里传来新闻播报声：

播音员：撒切尔夫人访华与邓小平会面，双方签署中英联合声明。彭定康发表最后施政报告。

唐龙：看来香港回归的日子不远了。

李飞：是啊，香港的未来会是个谜。我们只能希望最好。

两人沉默了一会儿，举杯相碰。

唐龙：珍重！

李飞：珍重！

两人道别后，各自离开。李飞去了海南，唐龙去了上海。

【香港背景音乐】

【男子低沉的旁白】

那时正值邓小平南巡讲话后，广东和海南的经济高速发展，但也催生了猖獗的走私活动。

李飞经营的是代理进口大宗产品业务，将国外钢材运送到海南。当地的不法商人利用国家给海南进口商品免税的政策，采取设立虚假项目报批手段，获取免税大宗商品进口批文。

将货物运到海南，免税清关后，再将货物偷运到广东湛江港口，从逃税中获取巨额利润。规模庞大，形成了一条龙的操作模式，港口、海关、商检、运输、公安都有参与进来，规模之庞大难以想象。

李飞之前一点不知情，但之后目睹了这一切并被卷入其中，险遭当地黑社会、不法商人以及腐败的公检法的毒手。在朋友帮助下脱险，随后，震惊全国的赖昌星走私案件爆发。

【场景结束】

【场景三十六】
港口交接

【外景　海南　1998 年】

【镜头】

伴随画外音，缓缓掠过三亚、海口的秀丽风光。

李飞从飞机上下来，与当地商人陈总相见。两人寒暄几句，陈总热情地邀请李飞去港口查看货物。

陈总：李总，您订购的几万吨钢材已经到达港口，正在卸货呢。货物堆得像山一样高，您放心，我们已经办完海关手续，很快就可以放货。

李飞：辛苦您了，陈总。

一行人来到港口，只见码头上堆满了钢材，工人们正忙着卸货。

陈总：李总，您看，这些都是您的钢材。

李飞：嗯，挺不错的。

陈总：海关手续已经办妥，我们马上就可以提货了。

李飞：好，那就麻烦您了，陈总。

【场景音乐】轻快的背景音乐，或者仅仅使用自然环境的声音来营造气氛。

【场景三十七】
夜色迷离

【内景　歌厅　夜晚】

镜头转到一个豪华的歌厅，李飞和陈总坐在包厢里，身边环绕着漂亮的陪酒小姐。

李飞：陈总，这次合作很愉快，我敬你一杯。

陈总：李总客气了，我应该敬您才是。

两人举杯畅饮，气氛一片祥和。

这时，一个手下匆匆走进包厢，附耳对陈总说：

手下：陈总，港口那边出了点问题，货物被海关扣留了。

陈总：脸色一变，李飞也察觉到了异样。

李飞：陈总，发生什么事了？

陈总：没什么，一点小问题，我马上让人去处理。

李飞：不用了，我自己去看看吧。

陈总：也好，我陪您一起去。

两人离开歌厅，赶往港口。

【场景音乐】舞厅音乐，伴随着欢快的节奏，掩盖着暗处的波涛汹涌。

【场景三十八】

海关纠纷

【地点】室内 / 海关 / 白天

【人物】

- 李飞：报关员
- 赖总：商人
- 关长
- 秘书

【场景描述】

李飞和赖总来到海关。赖总背着一个大包，试图直接进入关长办公室。

【对话】

赖总：这件小事找关长就能解决。你跟关长熟悉吗？不认识？去了就认识。

秘书：你好，请先预约。

赖总：我认识关长，我需要您的帮助。

说着，赖推开秘书，直接闯入关长办公室。

赖总：方关长，您好！

关长：你是？

赖总：您不认识我，我叫赖总。我请您帮忙，我的货物在海关遇到点问题，听说您能帮助我解决。

关长：你应该走正常手续解决。

赖放下手里的大包，打开拉链，露出里面一捆捆崭新的港币。

赖总：请关长多关照。

说着，赖拉着李飞退出办公室。

李飞（惊讶）：你搞定了？你都不认识他？

赖：没事，现在认识了。明天就可以放货。

李飞：等等，赖总，货款还没到呢。

赖：是这样，这次的货款是国外枫叶国家银行信用证付款，需要一点时间才能到账。你看能不能通融一下，先放货给我？

李飞：不行，这违反规定。无论是任何银行的款项，都必须是按照合同约定付款后才能放货。

赖：那怎么办？我的货很急，不能再耽误了。

李飞：你可以先去银行申请办理信用证议付，这样就可以尽快拿到货款。

赖：可是，这样一来，手续就太繁琐了，而且还要支付额外的费用。

李飞：没办法，这是规定。如果采取非法手段提货，将有可能触犯法律。

赖：（沉思）好吧，我再去想想办法。

李飞：嗯，你最好还是按照规定来办理。

旁白：李飞不知道，这次放货已经为他埋下了一个隐患。

【场景结束】

【场景三十九】
暗流涌动

【室外 / 港口 / 夜】

【音效】海浪拍打岸边，远处传来汽笛声

【场景】夜幕降临，港口灯火通明，巨大的货轮停靠在码头。李飞接到一个神秘电话，电话那头传来一个低沉的声音，告知他赖的人已经买通港口人员，将货物盗运走。

李飞（震惊）：什么？！不可能！

电话（阴笑）：你最好快点赶到港口，否则货物就永远消失了。

李飞（挂断电话，脸色凝重）：该死！

场景：李飞火速赶到港口，却发现货物已经一空。他意识到问题严重，只得选择报警。

警察（身穿黑色制服，戴着墨镜）：李先生，请详细说明情况。

李飞（焦急）：有人盗窃了我的货物，价值数千万美元！

警察（冷静）：请放心，我们会尽快追查凶手。

【场景】警察迅速展开调查，以盗窃罪追逃。与此同时，李飞也收到了来自对方的威胁，要他付出生命的代价。

画外音（低沉）：这就是李飞的工作环境，充满着危险和挑战。但他始终坚持自己的原则，不畏强权，勇于斗争。

画外音（叙述）：

枫叶国家银行当年在中国开展信用证进口贷款业务，由于不了解中国法律，数十亿美元贷款不受中国法律保护，最终血本无归，被迫撤离中国。

许多中国国企高层利用这一漏洞，疯狂贪污加拿大银行款项，许多私人公司也借此赖账不还，完成了他们原始资本积累，其中不乏耳熟能详的上市公司。

李飞当时也同样得到巨额贷款额度，但他为了遵守诚信，不让在银行工作的朋友为难，竭尽全力归还贷款，最终一无所得。

【场景】时间转眼到了 1998 年，走私活动愈演愈烈，已经到了疯狂的地步。李飞预感到，将有大事发生。

【音效】音乐逐渐变得紧张，预示着即将到来的风暴

【场景结束】

【场景四十】
逃离险境

【室内 / 宾馆 / 夜】

【音效】

电视播放香港回归的画面和声音，电话铃声

李飞坐在宾馆房间的沙发上，电视里播放着香港回归的盛况。他神情凝重，目光紧盯着屏幕，似乎陷入了沉思。

电话突然响起，打破了房间的宁静。李飞拿起电话，听筒里传来朋友焦急的声音：

"李飞，快跑！你可能有危险！"

"怎么回事？"李飞的心一下子提到了嗓子眼。

"走私的事暴露了，那些人买通了海关和公安，马上要来抓你和你的搭档。他们有可能杀人灭口，把走私的罪名栽赃到你们身上。你快离开，越快越好！"

李飞握紧了电话，额头上渗出细密的汗珠。他知道，朋友说的是真的，如果不及时离开，他很可能会死于非命。

"我现在就去机场。"李飞挂断电话，迅速收拾东西，离开了房间。

【场景四十一】

危机迫近

【室外 / 火车 / 船】

【音效】

汽车行驶的声音，火车鸣笛声，海浪拍打船舷的声音。

李飞和搭档在朋友的帮助下，乘汽车连夜逃离广东。一路上，他们心惊胆战，生怕被追捕的警察发现。

为了躲避追捕，他们辗转来到海边，租了一艘渔船，逃到了茫茫大海之上。

【画外音】

走私阴谋未能得逞，事情完全败露。走私分子、海关人员和腐败警察全部被抓获。这起震惊中国的湛江"9898"特大走私案，随后牵连出更大的赖昌星走私案件。险恶的经历，国企内部争权夺利的争斗，使得李飞心灰意冷，萌生了移民的想法。

【加拿大 / 美国 /1999 年】

【音效】

城市街道的声音

李飞站在加拿大的街头，看着眼前陌生的环境，心中感慨万千。

他终于离开了那个让他伤心的地方，开始了新的生活。

【画外音】

李飞在海外开始了新的生活，他将如何面对未来的挑战？他的命运又将何去何从？

【场景四十二】
异乡情怀

【镜头】李飞驾驶着汽车，窗外美加大地地标建筑和优美风景一一闪过。

【剧情】1999 年，李飞移民北美，开始了一段平静的生活。他游历于北美大陆，目睹了国外良好的生活和工作环境，内心深受震动，同时也感到些许迷茫。镜头闪过 XWave、SinoFox 在美国纽约交易所和纳斯达克上市的画面。

【背景音乐】2000 年美国加拿大流行音乐，如：

布兰妮·斯皮尔斯 -《Oops!...I Did It Again》

克里斯蒂娜·阿奎莱拉 -《Genie in a Bottle》

后街男孩 -《I Want It That Way》

NSYNC -《Bye Bye Bye》

加拿大天后夏奇拉 -《Whenever, Wherever》

【场景四十三】
赌城之夜

【场景】室内，拉斯维加斯，1999 年

【镜头】拉斯维加斯华丽的夜景闪过，李飞无所事事，来到赌城拉斯维加斯寻求放松和娱乐。

【剧情】此时，李飞遇到了来此度假的美国同学舒小萍及她的丈夫，以及另一位同学唐龙。唐龙已经在上海风生水起，成为当地的知名商人。他与多位企业家传出交往，被称为"商界精英"。他的公司业务繁荣，经常出入澳门和拉斯维加斯享受假期。

【场景】赌场内，唐龙与李飞等人一起欣赏表演和观赏美丽的建筑景观。

【背景音乐】选择中性的背景音乐，如：

- 迈克尔·布伦 -《Feelin' Good》
- 纳威·金 -《Smooth Operator》
- 乔治·迈克尔 -《Careless Whisper》
- 麦可·布雷斯 -《Sway》

【场景四十四】
重逢与别离

【室内 / 酒吧 / 拉斯维加斯】

舒晓萍、李飞、唐龙三个大学同学多年后在拉斯维加斯重逢，彼此都非常激动。加上舒晓萍的军官丈夫，四人一起在酒吧里畅饮，回忆往昔，气氛十分热烈。

随着酒量的增加，四个人的情绪也逐渐高涨起来。他们谈笑风生，欢声笑语，仿佛回到了大学时代。舒晓萍的军官丈夫也难得地放松下来，和三个人打成一片。

酒过三巡，四人已经微醺。舒晓萍和李飞轻松地交谈着，唐龙则闭上了眼睛，休息片刻。军官丈夫略显醉意，但还能保持清醒。

【室内 / 酒吧 / 拉斯维加斯】

【场景四十五】

紧急使命

【室内 / 酒店 /1999 年 / 拉斯维加斯】

深夜，舒晓萍和军官丈夫回到酒店房间。舒晓萍醉得人事不省，躺在床上呼呼大睡。军官丈夫帮她脱下鞋子和外套，盖好被子，然后准备去洗漱。

这时，军官丈夫的电话突然响起。他接起电话，听筒里传来一个焦急的声音。

"长官，南斯拉夫使馆发生紧急情况，需要您立即赶往五角大楼处理。"

军官丈夫脸色一变，挂断电话后迅速穿上衣服，离开了酒店房间。

【场景四十六】
外交风波

【地点】 室内 / 五角大楼 / 华盛顿

【时间】 1999 年

【人物】

- 舒晓萍军官丈夫（美方）
- 将军（美方）
- 陆程（中方）

【剧情】

镜头一： 飞机俯瞰五角大楼，画面逐渐拉近，进入五角大楼内部。

镜头二： 将军坐在办公桌前，表情凝重。舒晓萍军官丈夫站在他面前，情绪激动。

舒晓萍军官丈夫：将军，我不能相信这是误炸！中国大使馆怎么会被精确制导炸弹击中？这绝不可能是意外！

将军：我理解你的心情，上校。但我们已经调查过，确实是一次误炸。

舒晓萍军官丈夫：误炸？怎么可能？你们的情报系统难道如此不堪一击？还是说，你们故意针对中国大使馆？

将军：（沉默）我只能与总统保持一致。

镜头三：将军：执行命令。上校拿起电话，开始与中国军方联系。

镜头四：画面切换到北京国防部，陆程正在办公室工作。电话铃声响起，他接起电话。

陆程：你好，这里是中国国防部，我是陆程。

上校：你好，陆程。我是美国五角大楼。我代表美国政府，对中国驻南斯拉夫大使馆被误炸事件深表歉意。

陆程：（声音冷峻）贵方的道歉我们收到了。但我们无法接受"误炸"的说法。这起事件造成了严重后果，我们要求贵方进行彻底调查，并给予受害者应有的补偿。

镜头五：画面切换到电视画面，美国总统克林顿正在发表电视讲话，向中国人民道歉。

【旁白】

"1999 年 5 月 7 日，以美国为首的北约轰炸南斯拉夫，造成中国驻南斯拉夫大使馆被炸，三名中国记者不幸遇难。这一事件震惊了全世界，也深深地刺痛了中国人民的心。"

【地点】 北京 / 国防部

【时间】 1999 年 -2014 年

【人物】 陆程

【剧情】 陆程，大学军校毕业后返回北京进入军队国防部工作，最终升至大校。在他军旅生涯中，经历了大使馆被炸、中美撞机、香港回归驻军、911、台海危机、钓鱼岛事件，最后目睹军中腐败，一直到徐才厚、郭伯雄倒台。他与舒晓萍美国军官丈夫的交锋始终贯穿整部影片。

【旁白】 "陆程见证了中国军队在过去二十年的风风雨雨，也经历了中美关系的起起落落。他的故事，也是中国军队和中国崛起的故事。"

【场景四十七】

危机交锋

【地点】室内 / 空军司令部 / 北京 /2001 年

【人物】陆程、美国军人

【剧情】

空军司令部，突发中美飞机撞机事件，陆程与美国军人进行交涉。

【镜头】

1. 美国军人到访中国，陆程接待。

2. 陆程言辞交涉，据理力争。

3. 飞机被拆解运回的镜头。

【场景四十八】
911 的记忆

【地点】室内 / 酒店 /2001 年

【人物】陆程、美国军官托马斯

【剧情】

在一个清晨，陆程急匆匆地敲响了美国军官托马斯的酒店房间门。

【镜头】

托马斯打开门，面色惊愕，见到了陆程焦急的表情。

陆程：（慌张）托马斯，你必须看看电视，出事了！

托马斯：（不解）发生了什么？

陆程：（指向电视）打开凤凰卫视，快！

托马斯打开了电视，一条令人震惊的新闻在画面上展现——有关 911 的报道。

【画面：电视新闻报道显示着世贸中心大厦的恐怖袭击画面。】

托马斯：（震惊）这 ... 这怎么可能 ...

陆程看到了桌上的照片，发现了一个熟悉的面孔。

陆程：（心中一震）这个人是 ...

托马斯：（焦急）她在世贸中心 ...

陆程：（决然）让我帮你找到她。

陆程通过他的联系渠道，设法帮助托马斯与他的妻子联系上了。电话那头，托马斯听到了妻子的声音，情绪难以自持。

托马斯：（泣不成声）我会尽快回去，一切都会没事的。

陆程默默地退出了房间，留下了托马斯独自面对着电话中的妻子，他的内心也难以平静。

【场景四十八（加一）】

【剧情】美国攻打伊拉克，第二次海湾战争爆发。

【镜头】电视画面——国际新闻报道关于伊拉克局势的报道，议会辩论以及全球示威活动的画面飞速闪过。

【背景音乐】悬疑、紧张的音乐。

【场景四十九】
友谊与陨落

【室内 / 三里屯 / 北京 /2008 年】

【镜头】

镜头扫过 2008 年北京奥运会的热闹场面，李飞、舒小萍和陆程在北京相聚。他们游览北海，又在三里屯酒吧街畅饮。

李飞随后邀请舒晓萍，陆程在盘古七星酒店咖啡厅观看奥运圣火点燃，满天绚丽灿烂的烟花照亮了鸟巢，水立方，娘娘庙。

他们谈起唐龙在上海飞黄腾达的消息，众人感慨万千。

突然，传来消息：唐龙因涉嫌外汇诈骗案，被上海公安机关和检察院起诉。

【背景音乐】

【上海 /2009 年】

上海外滩夜景灯火辉煌，李飞和舒小萍赶到上海，希望能帮助唐龙，但最终无能为力。他们在法庭上目睹唐龙被判处 7 年有期徒刑。

【旁白】

唐龙被学校开除，出狱后在亲属的帮助下赴美留学，获得了硕士学位。

与舒晓萍在美国话别后，唐龙重返中国，前往上海经商。凭借着出色的外貌和口才，他很快在上海滩红极一时，成为赫赫有名的人物。他还与多位港台明星传出绯闻，其公司股票在上海上市，令他暴富。唐龙经常出入澳门和拉斯维加斯赌场豪赌，最终因诈骗等罪名再次被判入狱 7 年。

【旁白】

唐龙的公司股票"xx 科技"随后一落千丈，直至破产，被誉为中国史上最烂 A 股。唐龙至今仍在狱中服刑。

【场景五十】
审判时刻

【地点】 室内 / 法庭

【人物】

- 李飞
- 舒晓萍
- 法警
- 唐龙
- 陆程（电话中的声音）

李飞和舒小萍站在法庭旁，目睹着对唐龙的判决。法警将唐龙带入法庭，开庭审理，宣布判决。唐龙被戴上手铐，押解出庭。此时，李飞的手机响起，是陆程打来的电话。电话那头传来坏消息：杜雄在狱中不堪忍受折磨，越狱后在沙漠中被捕，押解途中死亡。

【场景结束】

【场景五十一】
绝望之境

【地点】室内 / 监狱 / 新疆 / 2010 年

【人物】

- 李飞
- 杜雄
- 狱警

李飞坐在飞机上，闭目养神，脑海中浮现出陆程的叙述。

陆程（画外音）： 杜雄在监狱受到了不公正的对待，他日复一日地遭受着狱中的困苦和折磨。他的心情愈发沉重，对未来充满了绝望。

【场景】监狱的院子，杜雄受到了狱警的粗暴对待。他眼神中充满愤怒，但却无能为力。

陆程（画外音）： 终于，杜雄忍无可忍，他决定寻找其他途径来维护自己的权益。

【场景】深夜，杜雄趁着狱警不注意，刺死狱警，然后逃出了监狱。

【背景音乐】紧张、压抑的音乐

【场景五十二】
逃亡与悲剧

【地点】 室外 / 沙漠 / 新疆

杜雄逃出监狱后，奋力穿越茫茫沙漠。他饥渴交加，筋疲力尽，在沙漠中漫步时，被追捕的警察发现了他。

【场景】 警察将杜雄拴在马尾拖回。

陆程（画外音）： 杜雄在沙漠中的逃亡被抓后死亡。

【背景音乐】 悲伤、凄凉的音乐

镜头再次回到北京

【场景】 李飞从回忆中清醒过来，他望着窗外，眼神中充满了复杂的表情。

【旁白】 杜雄的故事，让李飞陷入了沉思。他开始思考，自己的人生道路究竟应该如何选择。

【场景五十三】

往事如烟

【地点】室内 / 香山 / 北京 /2017 年

电影情节回到 2017 年的聚会场景。

【剧情】

一封快递送来了一封信，确认杜雄已经去世。

场景变得凝重，李飞的思绪被打断。镜头再次回到同学聚会。

女儿走进来："爸爸，你看起来心情不太好，发生了什么事？我看到了那封信。"

"爸爸，你曾提到过他，他犯了很多错误，最后因逃跑而去世。但每个人都会犯错，包括爸爸在内。有时候，改变命运只是一瞬间的事。"

女儿："你年轻时也犯过错，说给我听吧。"

李飞低下头，不敢直视女儿的目光，思绪飘向远方，犹豫一会儿才缓缓说道：

"那是在我和你妈妈结婚之前，我和一个朋友决定再次体验单身生活。"女儿："现在看来，这种做法已经不那么合适了。"

舒晓萍走过来，打破了他们的对话，"你们在讨论什么呢?"她递过来一封中国邮政的快递，"刚收到，唐龙已经出狱，他直接返回美国了。"李飞感到欣慰，为唐龙的自由而感朝气蓬勃。

几位同学围拢在一起，高兴地看着孩子们，幸福感洋溢在脸上。"我们已经老了，孩子们是未来的希望，他们是幸福的，没有我们儿时的贫困，但也没有我们儿时的经历，和天真无邪的快乐。"

此时，音乐突然停止，背景的电视屏幕开始播报新闻。

"国家正积极打击腐败，政府宣布一系列反腐措施，强调依法治国。"

大家一起聚精会神地关注着电视屏幕，目光凝重。新闻报道着一些国内政治动态。

"一些政府官员因违反法律被判刑。"

在这些新闻的背景下，大家陷入了沉思，思考着国家的未来和世界的局势。

【场景五十四】
突发事件

【地点】 室外 / 宴会厅门口

一位身着制服的警长走进宴会厅，众人迎上前去。

警长:"同学们，真抱歉！因为临时出现维稳任务，我无法准时参加聚会，只能抽出一会时间和大家见个面。"

众人纷纷围过来握手致意，寒暄问候。

【场景五十五】
告别与使命

【地点】室外 / 香山脚下

一辆挂着军牌的吉普车开进宴会厅院内。一名军人下车，将一封标记着"机密"的信件递交到陆程大校手中。

陆程拆开信，阅读后，对众同学说："同学们，很遗憾，我必须先离开了。刚刚接到上级紧急通知，近期美国战机频繁靠近我国南海领空侦查，为防止突发事件发生，需要加强领空监视。"

众同学纷纷向陆程大校表示理解和支持，相互握手，挥手告别。军车徐徐开向远方。

此时，一位中国快递工作人员递给李飞一封特快专递，李飞打开，是法院的最终判决书，内容涉及李飞与某水泥集团的股权纠纷。判决书确认了李飞持有该企业 20% 股权的事实（目前价值 2 亿人民币），但股权多次转让后，现已归属于一家国有企业。由于之前的诉讼主体不明确，法院驳回了李飞的上诉请求。

这是李飞意料中的结果。五年的漫长诉讼，经历了各级法院，李飞目睹了整个司法过程的复杂性与挑战，过程跌宕起伏，仿佛电影情节一般精彩。

尽管如此，李飞仍感到些许安慰，因为至少判决书确认了他的股权真实性。但他深知，与国有企业的法律对抗将会更加艰难，胜算渺茫。然而，李飞不会轻言放弃，他决定继续上诉，捍卫自己的合法权益。

李飞凝望远方，前路漫漫，他决心继续前行，挑战未知的未来。

【场景五十六】

珍贵的再见

【地点】 首都机场 / 候机楼

李飞、舒晓萍与前来送行的陆程等同学一一话别。

【场景五十七】

重逢与新时代

【**地点**】纽约肯尼迪机场

舒晓萍大校的丈夫带着孩子，热情地迎接她和李飞。他们拥抱在一起，祝贺同学聚会成功。舒晓萍激动万分。

机场电视正在播放新闻：

1. CNN：美国总统特朗普任命极右翼人物史蒂夫·班农为总统战略首席顾问。

2. FOX：美国总统将在海湖庄园会见到访的中国国家主席习近平。

3. CNBC：俄罗斯总统普京在克里米亚问题上采取行动，引发国际关注。

4. BBC：企业家马斯克宣布成功发射登火星计划火箭，特斯拉即将推出电动皮卡 Cybertruck。

5. 美国之音将有一场重磅采访。

最后一条新闻引起了李飞的注意。

【音乐响起】

【字幕拉开 ... END】

【背景音乐】

屏幕字幕出现，画外音开始叙述: "本片主要人物原型均为虚构故事人物。时代在前进，梦想在继续，生活将永远向前 ..."

【影片要点】

1.贯穿影片的背景音乐（包括中国、美国、加拿大、香港）以及歌曲、舞蹈要具有鲜明的时代特征，必须是脍炙人口、耳熟能详的。

2.人物对话简洁，除非必要，对话越少越好。有些场景无需对话，由画外音简单叙述。

3.一些场景镜头要体现各地名胜古迹、风景如画、视野开阔，既展现陈旧灰暗，又展现时尚潮流，各个时代特征明显。

4.画面紧凑，不拖泥水。无论是人物对话、殴斗、叙事等场面，要求语速节奏感强快。

5.取景拍摄城市：北京、上海、广州、深圳、海南、香港、拉斯维加斯、华盛顿、加拿大。城市多，预算高。

6.中文对话，英文字幕，翻译要求准确。

Synopsis of "The Dream of an Era"

◇ Screenwriter: Hai   January 2017

1. Overview

The Dream of an Era" is a period drama spanning 45 years, featuring fictional characters inspired by real people. The film's five protagonists—one woman and four men—are classmates from Class Two, Grade Five, at an elementary school in Beijing in 1972. The story follows the divergent life paths of Li Fei, Lu Cheng, Tang Long, Shu Xiaoping, and Du Xiong from 1972 to 2017, reflecting 45 years of social changes in China and the interweaving of its development with the outside world, highlighting the interplay between individual destinies and societal developments.

2. Structure

The film employs a dual narrative structure, primarily focusing on the story in China, with a secondary narrative in the United States. These two storylines intertwine and complement each other. The film uses a reverse chronology, starting with Nixon's visit to China in 1972 and progressing through to Obama leaving office and Trump being elected President in 2016.

3. Main Characters

Background and Personality

Li Fei grew up in a typical intellectual family. With a distinctive personality, he does not bully the weak, stands up for justice, and is unafraid of authority. He is keenly observant, sharp-minded, and well-rounded.

Youth

As a quintessential boy from a Beijing government compound, Li Fei experienced the turmoil of the late Cultural Revolution in the 1970s. His rebellious nature led him to defy norms, engage in fights, and pursued girls. He was close to his first love, his classmate Shu Xiaoping, and was curious about the outside world.

University Life

In 1980, Li Fei was admitted to Beijing XX College, which only accepted local students who would stay in Beijing after graduation. With no pressure to study, the campus atmosphere was somewhat lackluster. Li Fei didn't focus on academics; instead, he used his spare time to trade clothes and electronics in Guangdong, witnessing classmates being detained after attempting to flee to Hong Kong.

Entering Society

After graduation, Li Fei worked at a state-owned import-export company. From 1986, he frequently traveled to Shenzhen and Guangzhou, witnessing the opening of the Shenzhen Stock Exchange and participating in the Canton Trade Fair. He also engaged in import-export trade in Shanghai and Hainan.

In 1989, he returned to the University of International Business and Economics to study English and participated in the 1989 Tiananmen Square protests, narrowly escaping being shot.

Venturing into Business

Later, Li Fei traveled frequently to North America, the Middle East, Japan, Korea, Hong Kong, and Southeast Asia, dealing in bulk commodities like cement and steel.

In the early 1990s, he was stationed in Hong Kong as a chief representative, witnessing the entire process of Hong Kong's return to China in 1997.

Life Challenges

Li Fei experienced and got entangled in smuggling incidents in Hainan, Zhanjiang, and Fujian, making connections with the notorious Lai family smuggling group and nearly losing his life to organized crime and corrupt judicial systems.

Reflection and Rebirth

In 1997, disillusioned with internal power struggles in his state-owned company, Li Fei decided to move to Canada in 1999, traveling across North America to experience different lifestyles and cultures and enjoying a period of peace.

In 2005, Li Fei returned to China to start a new business venture. However, due to a series of unfortunate events, including the selection of the wrong partners, poor decision-making, and his own stubborn personality, several of his business investments fell short of expectations. He had once invested in a new type of cement project, acquiring a 20% stake. After going into production, the project's market value exceeded 1 billion RMB. As the project progressed, its value soared. Nevertheless, due to the complex local business environment and intense market competition, the project encountered numerous legal and regulatory challenges, ultimately leading to the infringement of the company's rights. Despite prolonged legal disputes, the case did not yield the desired outcome. During this period, he witnessed firsthand the various competitive tactics employed by state-owned enterprises and private enterprises in their struggle for resources and market share in the fiercely competitive market. This experience left him physically and mentally exhausted, and he developed a deep understanding of the challenges and uncertainties of the business world.

Li Fei's closest friend from university, Tang Long, was sentenced to years in prison for his involvement in commercial fraud case and is still incarcerated. His childhood companion, Du Xiong, also met a tragic fate, dying in prison after being shot attacking police officers under the influence of drugs. These experiences ultimately led Li Fei to awaken to the realities of life, prompting him to reassess his values and adopt a more detached perspective on fame and fortune.

Reviving Dreams

In 2015, Li Fei returned to Canada and conceived the idea of writing a film script to reflect on his 45-year journey and showcase China's development over the same period.

Ordinary yet Extraordinary

Li Fei's life was not marked by dramatic achievements or significant success, but his experiences spanned 45 years of China's societal evolution, witnessing many historical events and real-life characters. His sharp observation allowed him to reflect and encapsulate these in his script deeply.

Early Talent

Lu Cheng, a childhood friend of Li Fei, was tall and athletic, engaging in fights alongside Li Fei. He aspired to be a soldier and secretly loved their classmate Shu Xiaoping, but kept his feelings hidden.

Military Career

After high school, to alleviate the pain of unrequited love, Lu Cheng enrolled in a military academy outside Beijing, fulfilling his dream of becoming a soldier. Through rigorous training, he rose to a high-ranking position in the military.

Facing Challenges

Lu Cheng experienced significant events such as the Tiananmen Square protests in 1989, the bombing of the Chinese Embassy, the US-China aircraft collision incident, the 1997 Hong Kong handover military deployment, peacekeeping missions, Somali piracy escorts, and the Diaoyu Islands conflict. In all these events, he performed his duties fearlessly, making significant contributions to the country and its people.

US-China Negotiations

As a Chinese military representative, Lu Cheng was involved in negotiations with American counterparts, playing a crucial role in safeguarding national interests. He developed a professional relationship with David Thomas, an American officer who later married Shu

Xiaoping. Despite being adversaries, they maintained a collaborative relationship.

Early Achievements

Tang Long displayed exceptional business talent early on. Descended from a prominent family in Yunnan, he was tall, handsome, and skilled, once being a junior table tennis champion in Beijing. He and Li Fei delved into electronic and clothing trades, laying his business foundation.

Business Journey

In the commercial arenas of Beijing and Shenzhen, Tang Long and Li Fei struggled together, facing numerous ups and downs. Adventurous by nature, Tang Long once attempted to smuggle into Hong Kong (to the United States) but was intercepted.

Rise and Fall

Tang Long's life was fraught with challenges. He indulged in hedonistic pursuits and was frequently entangled in private parties. A private gathering led to his arrest and reeducation, resulting in a temporary loss of academic status. Nevertheless, his intelligence, charm, and table tennis skills, along with family support, enabled him to study in the U.S., where he earned a master's degree and became a U.S. citizen.

Business Peaks and Decline

In 2000 Returning to China, Tang Long thrived in Shanghai, marrying a well-connected actress and rapidly ascending in his career. However, his business empire crumbled due to poor management. Tang Long was implicated in a forex scam and sentenced to seven years in prison, marking one of China's most significant stock market failures.

Early Brilliance

Shu Xiaoping was intelligent and stunningly beautiful from a young age. She was Li Fei's first love and Lu Cheng's secret crush. Her beauty and academic excellence made her the object of admiration and competition among boys, often leading to conflicts.

Friendship and Love

During university, Shu Xiaoping was close to Li Fei and

Tang Long, sharing their youthful joys and sorrows. She narrowly escaped a dangerous situation at a questionable party, thanks to Li Fei. After graduation, her excellent grades earned her a place at an American university, where she married an American officer and settled in the US, becoming a senior manager at Cola King.

Intersecting Fates

Shu Xiaoping's husband worked at the Pentagon and was involved in many US-China conflicts. Meanwhile, she maintained a professional relationship with Lu Cheng at the Chinese Ministry of Defense. Despite their opposing roles, her influence fostered a productive collaboration, contributing to US-China relations.

Early Friendship

Du Xiong, Li Fei's childhood friend, came from a low-income family but possessed remarkable athletic talent, excelling in sprinting and football. Despite occasional conflicts, they became close friends.

Turning Point

Du Xiong joined the Beijing Junior Football Team but

left due to personality clashes with the coach. His life spiraled downward, with multiple detentions for fighting, eventually leading to reeducation through labor. Even after release, he led a wayward life, making a living through street vending, but his violent nature led to frequent altercations.

Friendship and Despair

Despite Li Fei's numerous attempts to help, Du Xiong's fate was unkind. He was imprisoned again for fighting and gradually became addicted to drugs. Despite Li Fei's efforts, Du Xiong died tragically during an escape attempt, ending a life of turmoil and despair.

Movie Opening Scene

[**Opening**] Beijing, 2017, Daytime, in a traditional Courtyard House

[**Scene**]

In a traditional courtyard house in Beijing, an old-fashioned telephone sits quietly on a table. Suddenly, the phone rings, breaking the silence of the room.

Li Fei (from behind):

Hello, this is Li Fei. "What? A reunion for our elementary school class after 45 years?"

[**Scene transitions quickly**]

Shanghai Bund

A woman (holding an American XPhone records a Vox-Celerate voice message):

Received, received. I'll definitely be there!

Guangzhou

A man, holding a Huaxin phone reads a China Connect

text message:

Alright, I'll be there on time!

Shenzhen - Digital Innovation Hub Building

A young man at a computer sees a QQ notification blinking and reads a message:

Awesome, I can't wait to see my old classmates!

New Zealand

A housewife at a MicroWindow computer reads an overseas email:

Great, I will definitely come back to attend!

Atlanta, USA - Cola King Headquarters Office

A female executive glances at her Apple Watch and reads a Facebook notification:

Good news! I'll be there for sure!

All screens freeze. A voice-over begins:

Voice-over: Attention to all classmates of fifth grade and second class, both at home and abroad: the forty-fifth-year reunion will be held in Xiangshan, Beijing.

Li Fei (from behind, murmuring to himself):

Forty-five years since graduation. How is everyone doing?

Subtitles appear: "The Dream of an Era" is a fictional film inspired by historical events, but all characters and plots are purely fictional.

[Song] Singing:

The east wind blows, the war drums beat,

Who in the world today fears whom?

It's not the people who fear the imperialists,

But the imperialists who fear the people!

[Subtitles and Narration]

In 1972, Chinese leader Mao Zedong invited President Richard Nixon to visit China, marking a new chapter in Sino-American relations.

China returned to the international stage, and the actions of these two great men demonstrated their foresight, profoundly influencing the political landscape of today's world.

China and the United have since become the most influential countries globally, jointly determining the future direction of world development.

The film begins with the visit of the U.S. table tennis team to China in 1972, followed by Nixon's visit, and unfolds through the life trajectories of five students, linking together significant historical events.

Key Events:

- Nixon's visit to China
- The late Cultural Revolution
- Tangshan earthquake
- Tiananmen Square incident
- Resumption of college entrance exams
- Reform and opening up, Crackdown on Pornography
- 1989 student movement
- Bombing of the Chinese embassy in Yugoslavia
- U.S.-China aircraft collision
- Hong Kong's return to China
- 911
- Beijing Olympics
- Diaoyu Islands dispute

- Libaba's listing in the U.S.
- U.S. President Trump's inauguration

In 2017, Obama stepped down, and the new U.S. President Trump took office. Libaba's market value soared to the top, and China's GDP approached that of the United States.

The first part of the film, covering the years 1972 to 1987, primarily focuses on the growth experiences of five classmates—Li Fei, Lu Cheng, Tang Long, Shu Xiaoping (female), and Du Xiong—from their elementary school days to their university years.

Key elements depicted include:

- The Huang Shuai anti-trend incident
- Scarcity of basic supplies
- Social unrest in the late Cultural Revolution
- The culture of residential compounds
- Street gang fights
- Romantic relationships among teenagers
- University life

[Scene One]

Immersed in Time: A Night in Beijing, 1972

[**Location**] Beijing / 1972 / Night / Inside a Classroom

[**Visuals**] A small room is furnished simply and modestly, bathed in dim, yellowish light. Portraits of Mao Zedong and political slogans hang on the walls, exuding the essence of that era.

[**Sound**] An old black-and-white television crackles with cacophonous sounds, displaying images of the U.S. table tennis team's visit to China. The athletes' peculiar outfits and hairstyles draw attention.

[**Narrator (Voice-over)**] In 1972, the Sino-American Table Tennis Friendship Tournament was held in Beijing. This was the first significant sports exchange between the two countries since 1949, marking a historic milestone.

[**Character**] A middle-aged man sits at a table, facing

away from the camera, softly narrating the social context of the time.

[**Background Music**] The faint strains of 'Sailing the Seas Depends on the Helmsman' blend with the visuals, enhancing the distinctive atmosphere of that era.

[Scene 2]

The Smoke of Elementary School Politics

[**Location**] Beijing / 1972 / Night (Daytime) / Inside a Residence (School)

Five classmates from Grade 5, Class 2: Li Fei, Lu Cheng, Long Yu, Shu Xiaoping (female), and Du Xiong, have been friends since childhood, playing together from a young age.

On this day in the classroom, the students are reciting political slogans about Nixon's visit to China, as instructed by their teacher. They feel confused about why the leader of the American "imperialists" is visiting and start asking the teacher various questions and making suggestions:

"Why invite the American imperialists? They are our enemies."

"Is it true that if we dig straight down, we'll reach America?"

"Can we arrest the American leader and hold a struggle session?"

"Can we shout anti-American slogans at Nixon?"

The teacher, flustered by the students' candid questions, repeatedly emphasizes that they must follow the directives from higher authorities and not engage in any inappropriate behavior. If any of Nixon's delegation or foreign journalists ask questions, students must answer according to the pre-approved scripts.

The students begin to recite along with the teacher: "American imperialist hegemony, unpopular with the people, defeated in the Vietnam War, with internal and external troubles, visiting our country..."

Children's voices rise and fall, and discipline begins to break down in the classroom, which is filled with laughter and innocent banter.

[**Film Scene**]

A primary school in Beijing, steeped in the thick atmosphere of the 1970s. A young, pretty teacher walks into the classroom.

Teacher: "Good morning, students. Please stand and greet the teacher."

The teacher hangs a globe on the blackboard.

Teacher: "Today we will have a special political lesson."

Pointing at China on the globe, she says:

Teacher: "You all know this is our great motherland, shaped like a majestic rooster. Actually, it used to look like a begonia leaf."

Realizing her slip, she quickly corrects herself:

Teacher: "A rooster, very grand."

Teacher: "Today, I want to ask if any of you know about America. Do you know where America is on the globe?

Raise your hand if you know."

The teacher begins calling on students:

Li Fei: "The United States is the largest imperialist country in the world and our enemy."

Lu Cheng: "American imperialists invaded Korea, and we defeated them in the Korean War."

Long Yu: "The imperialists occupy our precious island of Taiwan, helping Chiang Kai-shek block us from liberating Taiwan and unifying our motherland."

Shu Xiaoping: "We defeated the Japanese, but the Americans continue to support Japanese militarism."

Du Xiong: "The U.S. has the Ku Klux Klan, who persecute Black people."

The students start chanting slogans: "Down with American imperialism! U.S. out of Taiwan!"

The teacher praises, "You all have strong political awareness; very good! "

But today, I have an important announcement: We have received an urgent notice that the U.S. President is coming to visit China."

The students begin to chatter loudly. One student asks:

Student 1: "Teacher, why invite the American imperialists? They are our enemies."

Another student chimes in:

Student 2: "Isn't the U.S. President the biggest imperialist?

How can we let him visit?"

Another student interjects:

Student 3: "I heard America is beneath the earth; if we dig deep enough, we'll reach it."

The students start a heated discussion:

Student 4: "Will the American imperialists actually dig tunnels to attack China?"

Student 5: "How will the U.S. President come to China?"

Teacher: "They will come by plane."

Student 6: "Then can we arrest him and hold a struggle session as soon as he lands?"

The students burst into laughter.

Student 7: "Should we march in the streets to denounce American imperialism?"

The students leave their desks, banging on them and dancing, singing loudly:

"East wind blows, war drums pound, who fears who in the world now? It's not the people who fear the American imperialists, but the imperialists who fear the people.

Those who are righteous will have support, while those who are unjust will find little. The laws of history are irresistible; American imperialism is destined to perish, and the people of the world will surely triumph, the people of the world will surely triumph!

The atmosphere is charged with enthusiasm, and classroom discipline begins to unravel.

Teacher (loudly): "Quiet, students! According to higher authorities' directives, none of what you said is allowed. We must welcome the U.S. President's visit to China. This is a wise decision by Chairman Mao and the Central Committee. We must follow the directives and not engage in any inappropriate behavior."

The teacher then explains how to respond to potential questions from journalists:

Teacher: "If any of Nixon's delegation or foreign journalists ask you questions, how should you respond? You must follow the standard responses mandated by higher authorities. Every student must memorize the content."

The teacher begins writing on the blackboard, guiding

the students to read aloud together:

"American imperialist hegemony, disturbing the world, unpopular with the people, defeated in the Vietnam War, with no way out, coming to visit our country..."

Children's voices rise in unison. A sense of camaraderie and innocent curiosity fills the air as boys and girls whisper to each other, embodying a pure and unguarded feeling.

[Background Music]

(For detailed content, see the film script)

This scene highlights:

- The vivid 1970s school setting.
- The classroom's dark but tidy ambiance.
- The teacher calling on students by name.
- The teacher's youth, beauty, and intellectual demeanor.
- The students' simple, clean, and neat attire, wearing red scarves.
- Serious discussion topics presented humorously, reflecting the children's innocence and uninhibited speech.

- Distinctive characteristics of the five prominent students, four boys, and one girl.
- The complete recitation of the catchy slogans, and language reflecting the era.

[**Dance Focus**] The background music starts with "East wind blows, war drums pound," and the students begin dancing and singing with enthusiasm.

[Scene Three]

The Red Storm on the Streets: Beijing, 1972

[Beijing, 1972, Daytime, Street Scene]

[Camera]

- A panning shot sweeps across the streets of Beijing in 1972, revealing a flood of bicycles, dimly lit streets, and gray buildings.
- The crowd bustles with people who appear gaunt yet spirited. They wear gray clothing, simple yet tidy, exemplifying the distinctive characteristics of the era.
- The streets are lined with banners, loudspeakers blare criticism of the Italian director Antonioni's film "China."
- Revolutionary slogans such as "Down with Soviet Revisionism" and "Down with American Imperialism" occasionally ring out from the crowd

[Voiceover]

(Male voice, deep and powerful) In 1972, during the

Cultural Revolution, China was engulfed in a sea of red. People's thoughts and behaviors were strictly monitored, and anything that deviated from the official ideology was considered heretical.

[Background Music]

(For details, refer to the film script)

[Scene Four]

Diverse Lives During Nixon's Visit to China

[Night, Exterior]

The camera slowly pans across various households: government officials, bureaucrats, military families, traditional courtyard residences, crowded communal living quarters, and civilian neighborhoods—all depicting extreme poverty. People huddle together, intently watching an old, black-and-white.

[Visuals]

- In each household, people hold their bowls while squatting in the courtyard or sitting around the stove, listening to the radio broadcast about Nixon's visit to China.
- The television repeatedly shows Nixon disembarking from the plane and shaking hands with Chinese Premier Zhou Enlai: He waves, smiling broadly.

- At the Great Hall of the People, a welcoming banquet is held, with the band playing the American song "America the Beautiful."
- Chairman Mao Zedong shakes hands and converses with Nixon.

[Scene Details]

- Th camera captures snapshots of people's lives during that era:

  Some families live in cramped rooms, with adults and children crowded together for sleep, parents making every effort to shield their children from embarrassing situations.

  Police conduct household checks, demanding that individuals with questionable backgrounds leave Beijing immediately during Nixon's visit

  People use ration books, supplementary food coupons, and grain tickets to obtain food, reflecting the scarcity of essential goods.
- Some individuals watch the television and grumble, "It's such a shame, all that good Maotai and roast duck served to the head of the imperialists!" Their words are filled with dissatisfaction and incomprehension.

[Voiceover]

A deep male voice slowly narrates the historical context of the time...

[Background Music]

"Sailing the Seas Depends on the Helmsman, Revolution Depends on Mao Zedong Thought"

"Socialism is Good, the Communist Party is Good"

(Details... see the film script)

[Scene Five]

Class Reunion

[**Scene**] At the foot of Jade Spring Hill in Xiangshan, in a luxurious courtyard house, at dusk.

[**Time**] 2017

[**Characters**]

- Forty classmates from Grade 5, Class 2, around 55 years old
- Homeroom teacher
- Some classmates' children
- Family of an American classmate (via video)
- A relative of one classmate

[**Scene Description**]

The camera transitions to Beijing in 2017, where the Grade 5, Class 2 classmates are holding a reunion to celebrate their 45th graduation anniversary. Forty classmates, some in business suits, some well-dressed, others in luxurious attire, and some in casual wear, emerge from luxurious cars or walk to gather at this opulent courtyard at the foot of Jade Spring Hill.

The homeroom teacher stands at the entrance, accompanied by a few classmates, warmly welcoming everyone. After years apart, the classmates greet each other excitedly, reminiscing about their school days and fond memories.

Inside the banquet hall, the decor is lavish and modern. A large screen in the background plays 2017 news highlights: Xi Jinping meeting with Ma Ying-jeou, Libaba's IPO in New York, and China's GDP surpassing or approaching that of the United States.

After the main greetings, the central characters of the film enter the banquet hall. Though in their mid-fifties, they remain vibrant and elegant. A photographer captures the moments for posterity.

The focus of this scene is to showcase the reunion. The buffet table is laden with exquisite dishes. Classmates raise their glasses, chatting and laughing. Some have brought their children, introducing them to their old classmates. The young people are fashionably dressed, vibrant and full of life, contrasting with their parents' attire. They play with XPhones and dance Latin dances, savoring the joy of the reunion.

[**Special Scenes**]

- An American classmate's family sends a large bouquet via FedEx, and a video of the family of four congratulating their Beijing classmates plays on the big screen. The husband is a white American military officer with the rank of colonel.
- One classmate receives a letter from a relative, informing them that another classmate has passed away, the atmosphere suddenly turns somber and emotional. However, soon everyone resumes the celebration, continuing to enjoy the reunion.
- A disabled classmate, pushed in a wheelchair by his beautiful daughter, also joins the gathering.

[**Dances**]

- Old-fashioned ballroom dancing
- Young people's Latin dances: Salsa and Bachata

[Background Music]

"Time flies and never returns; memories can only be reminisced."

[Dialogue]

The dialogue should be concise and clear, emphasizing the lively atmosphere.

[Scene End]

The classmates spend a memorable evening filled with laughter and joy.

[Scene Six]

Revisiting Ideals

[**Time**] 1972

[**Location**] Grade 5, Class 2, School

[**Characters**] Teacher, Students

[**Scene Description**]

The camera shifts back to Grade 5, Class 2 in 1972. A group of students in simple clothing is energetically engaged in discussions. The boys are gathered together, talking about soccer, basketball, and which girl is the prettiest, speculating who might be dating whom. The girls, on the other hand, are whispering among themselves, secretly discussing their male and female classmates. Occasionally, a boy would tease the girls, prompting them to squeal "You rascal!" in mock anger, but they would respond playfully without genuine irritation.

One boy enthusiastically mimics a character from the model opera "Taking Tiger Mountain by Strategy," reciting in an exaggerated tone: "The Heavenly King covers the earth, the Pagoda suppresses the river demon!" which makes everyone burst into laughter.

At this moment, a familiar voice comes from the school broadcast, recounting the deeds of Huang Shuai, a student from Grade 5, Class 2. The broadcast repeatedly emphasizes: "I can still make a revolution without learning the ABCs. Studying is not important, Learning Mao Zedong Thought is what matters most."

The students buzz with discussion, as the school recently decided to implement open-book exams and introduced programs for learning from workers, peasants, and soldiers, inspired by the Zhang Tiesheng blank paper exam incident.

The class bell rings, and the teacher walks into the classroom to begin a lesson on ideals. The boys and girls quickly put away their playful demeanor, exchanging glances and passing notes. A few troublemakers begin to disrupt the class, disturbing the classroom order.

Today's lesson is on how to establish proper ideals. The students eagerly share their aspirations for the future.

Most of the students express their desire to become workers, peasants, or soldiers and to fight against American imperialists and Soviet revisionists.

A small, thin boy shyly says he wants to have a big house with many rooms so that his whole family doesn't have to sleep crowded together.

His remark immediately draws criticism from his classmates, who accuse him of bourgeois and revisionist thinking. They chant slogans: "Down with feudal, bourgeois and revisionist thinking! Down with revisionism!"

The teacher has to quickly asserting that students should have grander revolutionary ideals. They should remember that two-thirds of the world's people are still suffering, that African Americans in the U.S. are enduring hardships, and that Taiwan has not yet returned to the embrace of the great motherland. It is their duty to liberate them. The students cannot settle for the peasant's dream of "30 acres of land, a cow, a wife, and a warm bed."

A girl mentions that her father told her about an article in the Reference News, saying that Americans have invented a machine called an Fruit computer that can think like a human brain and write things.

No sooner had she finished speaking than her classmates jeered, accusing her of having Western-influenced thinking. A boy steals an apple from her bag, takes a bite, and throws it back to her, saying, "Is this what you use to think with?"

The whole class erupts in laughter. The girl, looking at the bitten apple, bursts into tears at her desk. (Close-up of the bitten apple.)

Another girl says she hopes to travel the world when she grows up, but she is immediately accused by her peers of wanting to defect to the enemy.

The girls are suddenly too scared to speak.

A boy, unable to stand it any longer, steps in to defend the girl, but this displeases a few of the troublemakers. They start a fight, shouting anti-establishment slogans, claiming that whoever has the strongest fists will be able to lead the revolution in the future.

[Background Music]

[Scene Analysis]

This scene portrays the unique era of 1972, showcasing the differing understandings and pursuits of ideals among the students in Grade 5, Class 2. They are full of aspirations for the future, yet constrained by the societal environment of the time.

[Scene Seven]

Exterior / Sports Field

[**Time**] Afternoon Break

(**The school bell rings, and students, like a flock of joyful birds, rush out of their classrooms and flood the sports field.**)

The boys, like wild horses that have broken free, bursting with energy, spread out across the field. Some are swinging baseball bats on the playground, playing with reckless abandon; others are chasing each other intensely on the basketball court, locked in fierce competition; still others battling it out on the soccer field, showcasing their agility and athletic prowess. The ping-pong balls fly back and forth, creating crisp sounds, rhythmic sounds, eliciting cheers from the spectators.

The girls gather on the other side, preparing for the upcoming school celebration. They are dressed in vibrant outfits, their faces glowing with youthful smiles. Some huddle in small groups, softly discussing the dance moves; others practice their singing earnestly under the guidance of the music teacher; and still others rehearse their dances on stage, their graceful movements like blooming flowers.

The entire sports field is filled with laughter and excitement, creating a lively and bustling atmosphere.

[Focus]

- Sports: By depicting the boys playing baseball, basketball, soccer, and ping-pong, this scene showcases the students' lively and healthy image.
- Choreography: The scene emphasizes the girls rehearsing their dances, highlighting their youthful vitality and artistic flair.
- Music: The music teacher's guidance and the girls' singing amplify the joyous and positive atmosphere.

[Scene Eight]

Air Raid Drill Turns into an Exercise

[**Time**] Night

[**Location**] Interiors

As a busy day comes to an end, the children bow to the statue of Mao Zedong before settling down to sleep.

At midnight, a sudden, urgent air raid siren blares, waking the children. Someone shouts that American planes are attacking, urging everyone to quickly enter the air raid shelters.

In a panic, everyone hurriedly dresses and rushes downstairs to the basement.

Meanwhile, neighbors begin to evacuate the children in an orderly fashion. Everyone calmly and systematically heads towards the air raid shelters, safely avoiding potential threats.

However, the subsequent loudspeaker announcement

reveals that this is just a drill. Some children realize they have put their pants on backward, which prompts laughter among the group.

Then, the loudspeaker blares the leader's latest directive: "Never forget class struggle," echoing through the streets. The children, now exhilarated, start a colorful flag parade down the street, creating a lively scene.

Boys and girls meet during the school parade, secretly holding hands.

On the street, a few people are paraded with tall hats and bound tightly, with the crowd shouting, "They are American spies, listening to Voice of America broadcasts." The crowd spits on them, and throws banana peels and eggshells at them; they are then taken away for a public denunciation. The scene is poignant.

A deep male voice narrates the societal context of the time, as scenes from the denunciation meetings flash by.

[Focus] Background Music

[Scene Nine]

Class Reunion in 2016

[**Time**] 2016

[**Location**] Xiangshan

[**Scene**] Luxurious interior and Exterior banquet

The camera transitions to the 2016 class reunion, the opulent modern banquet starkly contrasts with the simple scenes from 1972. Classmates toast each other, sharing laughter and lively conversation, creating a vibrant atmosphere. At this moment, the television news draws everyone's attention.

An Libaba executive, Qingyun, begins to recount how they raised the largest IPO funds in history in the United States and how they gained popularity among the American public. The television displays a smug-faced Obama and the intense debates between Trump and Hillary in the U.S. election.

The screen then switches to footage of Ma Ying-jeou

meeting Xi Jinping in Singapore, along with news about China's aircraft carrier and the Diaoyu Islands situation.

The banquet continues, remaining luxurious, warm, and full of enthusiasm. The male protagonist invites the female protagonist to dance. They look into each other's eyes, filled with affection, falling into a silent reminiscence of their beautiful past.

[**Background Music**] Soothing and romantic music

[**Detailed Description**]

The banquet scene could be described in more detail, for instance, with guests dressed in elegant attire, clinking glasses, and engaging in animated conversations.

When Qingyun talks about the IPO in the United States, specific details can be added, such as how he overcame difficulties and won the trust of investors.

The television news footage can be edited more tightly to enhance the dramatic effect.

When the male and female protagonists dance, incorporating body language and expressions can effectively showcase the evolution of their emotions.

Outrage

[Time] 1976

[Location] At the entrance of a middle school in Beijing

The scene shifts to the school gate, where students emerge in groups, chatting warmly and smiling brightly. They have grown up, with the girls looking graceful and youthful.

A crowd gathers at the gate, talking, some smoking and others whistling. Suddenly, they notice a frail girl named Shu Xiaoping. Several students approach her, scrutinizing her.

Shu Xiaoping feels uneasy and tries to break free, but to no avail. At this moment, Li Fei, Lu Cheng, and Du Xiong see the situation and immediately step forward to help Shu Xiaoping out of her predicament.

Li Fei and Lu Cheng calmly persuade the students to leave. Du Xiong picks up a stone from the ground but does not use it. The students gradually understand the situation and eventually leave.

With the help of other classmates, Li Fei successfully guides Shu Xiaoping out of the crowd. They have escaped potential danger but still feel unsettled.

[**Background Music**] Dramatic and tense

[Scene Eleven]

Exterior / Night / Park

[Scene Description]

As night falls, the park is quiet, with only the dim streetlights flickering softly. The shadows of trees dance gently, the fragrance of flowers fills the air, creating a romantic ambiance. The male and female protagonists stroll along the tree-lined path, their silhouettes elongated. The male protagonist is handsome and charming, while the female protagonist is beautiful and captivating. They converse softly, their faces radiant with happiness.

[Character Actions]

The male protagonist suddenly stops in his tracks, turns around, and gazes affectionately at the female protagonist. She also stops, their eyes meeting, filled with love for each other.

[Character Dialogue]

Male Protagonist: (earnestly) I love you, Xiaoping.

Female Protagonist: (emotionally) I love you too, Fei.

Male Protagonist: (leaning in to kiss the female protagonist)

[Scene Change]

Suddenly, several members of the workers' militia wielding clubs rush out of the darkness, surrounding the couple.

[Character Actions]

Workers' Militia: (shouting) In love? This is a park, not a place for your romance!

Male Protagonist: (surprised) We are in dating.

Workers' Militia: (angrily) In dating ? This is a park, not a place for your romance!

[Scene Change]

The workers' militia roughly shoves the male and female protagonists, taking them to the workers' propaganda team.

[Scene End]

Scene Twelve: Interior / Headquarters of the Workers' Propaganda Team

The atmosphere in the interrogation room is tense, dimly lit, and filled with a sense of oppression.

[Voiceover]

In those dark days, interrogations at the Workers' Propaganda Team headquarters often occurred in the dead of night, where people's fates were decided. A young girl, taken home by her parents, bears a face marked by complex emotions.

[Scene Thirteen]

Exterior / On the Street

Li Fei is walking home alone when he is suddenly attacked. Severely injured, he struggles to crawl back home. Upon hearing about Li Fei's injuries, a classmate immediately informs Shu Xiaoping. Despite her parents' objections, Shu Xiaoping resolutely rushes out to where Li Fei is.

Shu Xiaoping supports Li Fei as they make their way back home, anxiously tending to his wounds. They embrace tightly, expressing their mutual care and concern. They share a kiss, ready to face the challenges of the future together.

[Scene Fourteen (1)]

Exterior / On the Street

Li Fei and Du Xiong rally a group of people, preparing for revenge. The scene transitions to the entrance of a courtyard, where two groups stand off against each other, armed with makeshift weapons, emotions running high, and a fight on the verge of breaking out. Suddenly, one person attempts to charge forward, causing chaos, but is quickly restrained by others. The crowd is composed of individuals in various outfits representing different social groups. The scene shifts to a standoff, with people distributing Yongheng-brand cigarettes, expressing their demands and opinions instead of distributing weapons. The scene of weapon distribution is omitted. Police arrive in vehicles, quelling the chaotic situation without any intense conflict. The background music creates a tense atmosphere but does not escalate the violence.

[Era's Typical Characteristics]

Li Fei and Du Xiong gather people to begin their

retaliation, creating a tense scene.

Camera: At the courtyard entrance, two groups face off, armed with makeshift weapons.

The fight begins to escalate into a brawl.

In the scene of the standoff, each courtyard features distinct, organized uniforms.

Navy, Army, Air Force, government compounds, and residential areas each have unique outfits,

Sheep wool caps, military belts, and white masks are visible.

Groups distribute cigarettes according to their different factions.

The scene is spectacular and filled with tension, just as the conflict is about to erupt,

Police on jeeps, motorcycles, and bicycles suddenly appear,

The crowd panics and scatters.

[**Background music**] sets the tense atmosphere.

[Scene Fourteen (2)]

Exterior / Street

[**Location**] Interiors / Police Station

[**Characters**]

- Li Fei: Male protagonist, teenager
- Shu Xiaoping: Female protagonist, teenager
- Police Officers: Two middle-aged men

[**Scene Description**]

Li Fei and Shu Xiaoping are taken to the police station, where two police officers are questioning them.

Police Officer 1 (speaking in dialect): "What were you doing in the park? Explain yourselves clearly."

Li Fei and Shu Xiaoping hold each other's hands tightly, their eyes resolute, unwilling to elaborate on their private matters.

Li Fei: "We didn't do anything illegal."

Shu Xiaoping: "We are innocent."

Seeing their determination, the police officers have no choice but to let them go.

Li Fei (as they walk out of the police station, holding Shu Xiaoping's hand): "Thank you!"

Shu Xiaoping: "We're facing this together; there's nothing to fear."

Li Fei: "We will not bow to unjust treatment."

[**Voiceover**] Classmate Du Xiong was sentenced to three years of re-education through labor.

A deep male voice narrates: "The social turmoil at that time, with scenes from public trials flashing by."

[**Visuals**] On the street, loudspeakers blare commentary on the film "China" shot by an Italian photographer.

[**Voiceover**] Social unrest, ideological confusion, material scarcity; people are waiting for significant change.

[**Background Music**] Melancholic and oppressive music

[**Visuals**] In the streets and alleys, various rhymes and tunes are being shared among the people. The rhyme goes: "Knife boards and belts, inside and outside the waist; spinning wheels and daggers, the brothers have it all. Ready to brawl, at Dongdan, Xisi, in front of the Drum Tower, the back gate of Beihai, the Summer Palace..."

[Voiceover] In those turbulent times, people expressed their struggles against life and their hopes for the future in their own ways.

[Scene End]

Dawn Breaks, Earthquake Strikes

[**Scene**] Interior and Exterior

[**Time**] Dawn

[**Sound Effects**] The serene chirping of birds is gradually replaced by a distant, faint rumbling.

[**Visuals**]

- Rays of sunlight filter through the curtains, illuminating the modest room.
- Inside, a family of three sits around the dining table, enjoying a simple breakfast.
- The father wears a content smile, while the mother gently serves porridge to the child, who innocently plays with a toy.
- Outside, birds sing joyfully, and flowers sway gently in the breeze. Everything is peaceful and harmonious.

[**Voiceover**] "July 28, 1976, Tangshan—a typical dawn."

[**Sound Effects**] The rumbling grows closer and louder, like a roar from the depths of hell.

[**Visuals**]

- Suddenly, the scene begins to shake violently. The house creaks and groans, and furniture topples over.
- The family of three stands up in terror, but before they can react, the ceiling crashes down, and rubble rains down upon them.
- Screams pierce the tranquil morning, plunging everything into chaos and darkness.

[**Background Music**] Tense, urgent music accentuates the suddenness and ferocity of the earthquake.

[Scene Sixteen]

Tiananmen Square, Resonant Recitation

[Scene] Exterior, Tiananmen Square

[Time] Daytime

[Visuals]

- Tiananmen Square is filled with a sea of people, their dark forms merging into a vast ocean of red.
- A gigantic portrait of Chairman Mao Zedong hangs above Tiananmen Gate, his expression solemn yet benevolent.
- Amidst the crowd, a young man stands in front of the monument, holding up a book of Mao's quotations, his voice booming as he recites: "I hear the ghosts cry, I weep while the wolves laugh, mourning tears for the heroes, as the sword is drawn!"

[Sound Effects] The passionate recitation resonates throughout the square.

[**Visuals**] As night falls, the crowd becomes agitated, and a large number of workers' militias emerge, surrounding the area from Tiananmen, the Great Hall of the People, the National Museum of China, and Qianmen Street. The camera shifts to the masses of workers' militia, holding batons, marching resolutely. Deng Xiaoping is ousted once again, becoming the scapegoat.

[**Voiceover**] On September 9, 1976, Chairman Mao Zedong passed away, and the nation mourned. Simultaneously, the Gang of Four was crushed, marking a new historical turning point for China.

[**Background Music**] Solemn and stirring music intertwines with the sorrow and hope of the era.

[Scene Seventeen]

Farewells and New Beginnings

[**Scene**] Exterior / Reeducation Center / University

[**Visuals**] The young boys and girls, with tears in their eyes, bid a poignant farewell. They have just visited their classmate, Du Xiong, at the reeducation center, leaving them with a swirl of emotions. After saying their goodbyes, they go their separate ways, stepping through the gates of their respective universities.

[**Scene Transition**] The camera transitions to scenes of various universities and military academies as students arrive and check in for their first day. Their faces radiate youthful energy and a sense of optimism about the future.

[**Background Music**] The rousing music gradually fades away, giving way to a soothing melody that seems to narrate the passage of time.

[**Voiceover**] Amidst the tears of farewell, they embark on new journeys, each carrying hopes and dreams in their hearts. As the times change, so do they, growing and evolving with each passing day.

[Scene Eighteen]

[Scene Eighteen]
Tremendous Social Change

The film begins by depicting the state of universities and society in China from 1977 to 1986.

From 1977 to 1986, China underwent significant social transformations. The reform of the university admission system and the reinstatement of the college entrance examination (gaokao) allowed a large number of young students to return to campus, injecting fresh vitality into the country's development. Meanwhile, China's doors gradually opened to the outside world, and Western culture and ideas began to flow in, challenging traditional societal norms.

[Scene Transition]

The scene shifts to show vibrant students on campus, attentively listening in classrooms and sweating on the sports field. A voiceover explains the educational reforms and social changes of this period.

[Interior/Family/Night]

At night, lights glow in every household. Black-and-white televisions in various homes are showing Japanese movies, featuring bustling streets and elegant clothing, which evoke curiosity and astonishment in viewers.

[Sound Effects]

The movie's theme song melodiously resonates throughout the room, creating an atmosphere of novelty and slight unease.

[Scene Transition]

On the TV screen, intense gunfight scenes from an American movie transport the audience to another world. The protagonist's bravery and fearlessness stir the blood of many young viewers.

[Background Music]

Following this, the movie's music transitions to a soothing melody, complementing the scenes on the TV that showcase Western culture.

[Scene Transition]

Some scenes in the movie make parents uneasy, prompting them to turn off the TV and send their children to bed.

[Sound Effects]

In the household, the tape recorder plays popular songs from Hong Kong and Taiwan, such as Teresa Teng's "When Will You Return?" and "Small Town Story."

[Voiceover]

The doors to the world have opened and cannot be closed again. That night, many people toss and turn, unable to confine themselves to their small worlds any longer. The outside world has opened its doors, and they are eager to explore and experience it.

[Background Music]

The soothing melody continues as the scene gradually fades, showcasing endless hopes for the future.

[Scene Nineteen]

University Dance

[Interior/Dormitory/University]

[Time] Evening

[Characters]

* Female Lead: Shu Xiaoping, a Chinese literature student, lively and cheerful, with a curiosity for new experiences.
* Best Friend: Wang Xiaomei, an English major, fashionable and avant-garde, daring to challenge traditions.
* Male Classmate 1: Li Fei, an architecture student, sunny and handsome, passionate about sports.
* Male Classmate 2: Tang Long, an economics student, humorous and talented.

[Scene Description]

As the music plays, the university dance is in full swing, with young students exuberantly expressing their youthful vitality. Shu Xiaoping and Wang Xiaomei, dressed in vibrant dresses, dance gracefully with Li Fei and Tang Long. Their faces radiate happiness, immersed in the joyous atmosphere.

In the dormitory, several classmates gather around the television, watching the news. The screen depicts the smoky scenes of the 1979 Sino-Vietnamese War, the shocking assassination attempt on American president in 1981, Maradona's glorious moments in 1982, and the tense backdrop of the Falklands War in 1984, all flashing by one after another.

Meanwhile, various advertisements flash on the TV, with catchy slogans showcasing brands like Tanaka Motors, Burger Town, and Cola King, illustrating the impact of the capitalist lifestyle.

Suddenly, the TV screen switches to news from the 1984 Los Angeles Olympics, where Chinese athlete Mr. Xu wins the gold medal in the men's 50-meter pistol event, marking China's first Olympic gold medal in history! The classmates erupt with excitement, cheering and celebrating this historic moment in various ways.

[Background Music]

Disco music and classic hits from the era alternate, creating a joyful and energetic atmosphere.

[Scene Twenty]

Skipping School to Shenzhen

[Exterior / Guangzhou / 1984]

[Time] Daytime

[Characters]

Male Lead 1: Li Fei, who, after graduating from high school and entering Beijing XX University, becomes disillusioned with his studies. Along with his like-minded classmate, Male Lead 3: Tang Long, they decide to skip school and travel to Shenzhen to trade electronic watches, T-shirts, and other goods, planning to sell them back in Beijing.

[Scene Description]

Li Fei and Tang Long stand on the platform of Guangzhou Railway Station, preparing to board a train to Shenzhen. Their eyes are filled with anticipation and excitement— this is their first time skipping school and their first trip to the South.

The train travels southward, the scenery outside the window flashing by. Li Fei and Tang Long gaze out at the landscape, their minds racing with thoughts. They dream of Shenzhen's prosperity and aspire to create wealth with their own hands.

Finally, the train arrives in Shenzhen. Li Fei and Tang Long disembark, awestruck by the towering skyscrapers before them. They take a deep breath and stride confidently into this city brimming with opportunities.

[Scene Visuals]

- The scene at the Shenzhen Luohu border, particularly the "China-Britain Street."
- The streets are crowded with bustling activity, displaying a wide array of goods.
- Li Fei and Tang Long weaving through the crowd, searching for business opportunities.

[Background Music]

Popular 1980s music, including Cantonese songs.

[Scene 21]

The Road of Hardship - The Struggles of Detention

[Interior / Detention Center / Shenzhen]

Li Fei discovers a note left by Tang Long and learns that he has gone missing. Overcome with anxiety, Li Fei immediately calls the police for help. After a thorough investigation, Li Fei finally learns of Tang Long's whereabouts: he was lured by locals into attempting to smuggle himself into Hong Kong and go to the USA, where he was intercepted by the Hong Kong police and deported back to China, and is now being held by the Public Security Bureau.

Li Fei, in a state of panic, rushes to the detention center to visit Tang Long. However, the sight before him is shocking: the conditions in the detention center are overwhelming and suffocating.

[Camera Shot]

The detention center. The crowded room is filled with many people, the air thick and suffocating. Li Fei sees Tang Long, whose eyes are filled with anxiety and exhaustion.

Li Fei, witnessing all this, feels a deep sense of powerlessness. He tries to plead with the guards, but ultimately his efforts are in vain.

[Background Music]

As sorrowful music plays, Li Fei can only return to Beijing alone.

[Scene 22]

Glory and Dreams - The Struggle Years of Guoqiang Appliance

[Exterior / Overseas Personnel Service Department / Beijing]

After returning to school, Li Fei continues to use his spare time to make extra money by reselling appliances in front of the Overseas Personnel Service Department. It is here that he meets the Huang brothers, who are also from Guangdong. The three often gather to exchange ideas, resell appliances, and chat about life. However, due to academic commitments and other factors, Li Fei ultimately cannot continue this side business.

[Voiceover]

In those days, many people from the Ministry of Foreign Trade were sent abroad on official assignments. According to national regulations, long-term overseas personnel could purchase some appliances, with an annual quota of four large and eight small items. Some families didn't need these appliances and sold them to resellers like Li Fei. Initially, most of these resellers were locals from Beijing, but gradually more people from other regions joined, primarily from Guangdong. They were among the pioneers of China's imported appliance trade, a hallmark of that era.

[Exterior / Fuchengmenwai Street No. 1 / Beijing]

Friends from Guangdong always surrounded Li Fei, conversing in their dialect. Sometimes, he felt impatient, but he understood that this was a communication barrier. However, the Huang brothers were exceptionally courteous; they offered cigarettes to all the appliance resellers every day, demonstrating their goodwill and friendliness.

[Camera Shot]

Founding of "Guoqiang Appliance"

On the screen, the Huang brothers stand in front of the Guoqiang Appliance store, beaming with smiles. From initially reselling appliances on the streets, they grew into one of the leading enterprises in China's home appliance retail industry. Their story has also become a reflection of China's era of reform and opening up.

Lost Youth

[**Location**] Interior / Dance Party / Beijing

[**Characters**]

- Tang Long: Male protagonist who returns to school after being released, hiding his situation.
- Li Fei: Second male lead, Tang Long's classmate.
- Shu Xiaoping: Female protagonist, elementary school classmate of Tang Long and Li Fei.
- Female Classmate: A girl Tang Long invites to the dance party.

[**Scene Description**]

At the dimly lit dance party, the music blares deafeningly as couples dance wildly under the ambiguous lights. Tang Long, Li Fei, Shu Xiaoping, and another female classmate are immersed in this hedonistic revelry.

Tang Long, having given up on himself, indulges in this

hedonistic lifestyle, frequently attending privately hosted questionable party. He invites Li Fei and Shu Xiaoping to join, unaware of the inherent risks.

Tonight, they attend a private dance party. The four classmates unleash their pent-up emotions on the dance floor, but gradually start to argue. Li Fei and Shu Xiaoping want to leave, but Tang Long insists on staying, while the other female classmate remains hesitant.

Suddenly, a public telephone rings, and Shu Xiaoping answers a call from Lu Cheng, who is far away at a military academy. She becomes emotional, her voice choking with tears. At that moment, the dance hall lights suddenly go out, followed by screams from both men and women, plunging the scene into chaos.

In a critical moment, Li Fei throws punches at several men lunging towards Shu Xiaoping to protect her and pulls her out of the dance hall. Meanwhile, Tang Long and the other female classmate are caught up in the chaos. Someone reports the party, and the police arrive unexpectedly, arresting Tang Long.

[Highlights]

[Dance] (Select the appropriate dance type based on the specific scene.)

[Background Music] Upbeat dance tracks with a strong rhythm to create a festive atmosphere.

[Scene 24]

The Judgment

[**Location**] Interior / Courtroom

[**Characters**]

* Judge
* Tang Long
* Lawyer
* Li Fei and Shu Xiaoping in the gallery

[**Scene Description**]

The camera shifts to the courtroom, where the judge announces the verdict: Tang Long is sentenced to six months in prison for his involvement in an illegal gathering and is expelled from school.

Li Fei and Shu Xiaoping, seated in the gallery, witness Tang Long's sentencing, their hearts filled with sorrow and reflection. The beautiful moments they once shared are now shattered by the harsh reality of the judgment, leaving them deeply heartbroken.

[Scene 25]

Longing at the Military Academy

[**Location**] Guilin Military Academy, Exteriors

[**Characters**]

- Male 2 (Lu Cheng): A cadet at the military academy who receives a letter from Shu Xiaoping informing him of Tang Long's imprisonment. He has secretly harbored feelings for Shu Xiaoping but has kept them to himself. He is also a close friend of Li Fei.

- Shu Xiaoping: The object of Lu Cheng's affection, who sends him a letter about Tang Long's situation.

[**Scene Description**]

Lu Cheng is engaged in serious military training on the grounds of the Guilin Military Academy. Sunlight filters through the treetops, casting a glow on his tall, upright figure, highlighting his resolute demeanor. Suddenly, a comrade hands him a letter from Shu Xiaoping. Lu Cheng's heart skips a beat, and he hurriedly opens it, learning about Tang Long's imprisonment. His brows furrow deeply, and he feels an indescribable pain welling up inside.

During a break in the demanding training, Lu Cheng secretly takes out Shu Xiaoping's letter and reads it carefully. Every word in the letter feels as though she is speaking directly to him, causing his emotions to surge. However, he is acutely aware of the distance between himself and Shu Xiaoping. To ease the emotional turmoil within, he resolves to throw himself even more into his military training.

[Plot Development]

- The grand spectacle of the military parade showcases the cadets' impressive bearing.
- The harsh training environment of the military academy highlights Lu Cheng's indomitable spirit and the ironclad yet tender nature of a soldier.

[Background Music]

Stirring military music begins to swell, intertwining with the scenes, highlighting the lofty aspirations and heroic spirit of the soldiers.

[Scene 26]

The Road of Adversity - From Prison to Football Field

[Exterior / Beijing]

[Time] Late 1980s

[Scene]

1. Release from Prison

Du Xiong, a man in his early twenties, with a lean build and a glint of intensity in his eyes, walks out of the prison gates with heavy steps. He takes a deep breath of the fresh air of freedom, yet feels lost and helpless.

2. Watermelon Stand

Du Xiong sets up a watermelon stand at a street corner. He shouts energetically to attract customers, but business is poor. As he watches the bustling crowd pass by, a sense of frustration wells up inside him.

3. Playing Football

Li Fei, a man in his early twenties and a university student with a passion for football, sees Du Xiong and approaches him to invite him to join a game. Du Xiong hesitates for a moment but eventually agrees.

[Scene Transition]

Quick flashes of scenes: Du Xiong leaving prison, setting up the watermelon stand, and playing football.

[Background Music]

Stirring music gradually rises, intertwining with the scenes, reflecting Du Xiong's inner struggles and desires.

[Narrator]

As time moved into the late 1980s, classmates went their separate ways after graduating from university, while Du Xiong ended up in prison for fighting. Upon his release, he had no stable job and had to make a living by selling watermelons. Li Fei, unwilling to see him give up on life, frequently invited him to join football matches. On the football field, Du Xiong rediscovered a long-lost sense of joy and confidence, and gradually began to reflect on his past behavior.

[End of Scene]

The End of "*The Dreams of an Era*" Part One

"The Dreams of an Era" Part Two

After graduating from university, Li Fei joined a state-owned enterprise and was later assigned to work in Hong Kong. In the early 1990s, he began importing bulk commodities in Guangdong and Hainan. This experience allowed him to witness firsthand the return of Hong Kong to China in 1997, as well as the rampant smuggling of imported goods during that time. He also befriended members of the notorious Lai syndicate, who would later gain infamy both domestically and internationally, narrowly escaping death at the hands of organized crime and corrupt law enforcement.

The dangers he encountered in business dealings, coupled with the complex interpersonal dynamics of state-owned enterprises, left Li Fei feeling profoundly disillusioned and contemplating leaving. He chose to immigrate abroad, leaving a deep impression due to the favorable living and working conditions. However, he also felt lost and disoriented abroad. Ultimately, he returned to China in 2005 and embarked on a new entrepreneurial venture.

[Scene 27]

Touching the Pulse of Reform at the Guangzhou Export Fair

[**Location**] Exterior, Guangzhou/Shenzhen

[**Time**] Daytime

[**Character**] Li Fei

[**Plot**]

Li Fei is taking his first flight to attend the Guangzhou Export Fair, where the venue is packed with people and buzzing with excitement. A dazzling array of goods is on display, with merchants from around the world jostling against each other, haggling over prices. Li Fei is overwhelmed by the scene, feeling the powerful tide of reform and opening up. Li Fei also witnesses the opening of the Shenzhen Stock Exchange, where the trading floor is bustling with activity, and people are rushing to the counters to make trades. Li Fei feels a sense of unfamiliarity amidst the crowd.

A Closed Friendship – The Beijing Friendship Store Incident

[**Location**] Interior and Exterior, Friendship Store, Beijing

[**Time**] Daytime

[**Characters**] Li Fei, Gatekeeper

[**Plot**]

Upon returning to Beijing from Guangzhou, Li Fei hears that the Beijing Friendship Store sells imported goods and eagerly heads there. However, upon arriving at the entrance, he is stopped by the gatekeeper, who informs him that only foreigners are allowed inside.

Li Fei is instantly filled with rage, pointing at the gatekeeper and shouting, "Do you think this is the Shanghai International Settlement? Why can't Chinese people go in?!" With that, he pushes past the gatekeeper and storms into the store.

Seeing the commotion, the store staff immediately steps in to stop Li Fei and calls the police, who take him to the station. After some explanation and a brief education, Li Fei is eventually released.

Farewell and Destiny: Shu Xiaoping's Romance Abroad

[Location] Interior / Capital Airport

Li Fei rushes to the airport to bid farewell to Shu Xiaoping alongside Lu Cheng, as Tang Long is about to leave for the United States for his studies.

Airport Announcement:

"Passengers on flight XX to New York, USA, please proceed to the gate."

Tearful Farewell

Shu Xiaoping and Tang Long share a tearful farewell, waving goodbye to Lu Cheng.

[Background Music]

As the music begins, the camera transitions to the United States.

[United States]

Shu Xiaoping and Tang Long begin their study-abroad life.

[New York Manhattan]

The camera briefly captures the Twin Towers in Manhattan, New York.

Background music plays (replace with proprietary music).

[Campus Café]

Shu Xiaoping meets and falls in love with an American officer at the school café, eventually marrying him. This American officer works at the Pentagon.

[Shu Xiaoping's Charm]

Shu Xiaoping has been a school star since childhood—intelligent and beautiful, always the object of boys' affection. During her university years, she became the belle of many dances and almost got caught up in a questionable party.

[Twists of Fate]

The American officer Shu Xiaoping marries later forms a

strong professional relationship with Lu Cheng, who now works for the Chinese military's Ministry of Defense. They collaborate and sometimes clash, but neither initially realizes that the American officer has married Lu Cheng's former secret crush.

Debating the Korean War - The Sino-American Dispute

[**Location**] American University Classroom

[**Time**] 1987

[**Characters**]

- Professor
- American Students
- Shu Xiaoping
- American Officer

[**Scene Description**]

Professor: Class, today we're going to discuss a very important topic: the impact of the Korean War on Sino-American relations.

American Student 1: I believe it was North Korea that initiated the war, and the United States intervened based on a United Nations resolution.

American Student 2: I agree. The United States' actions were in defense of democracy.

Shu Xiaoping: I have a different perspective. I think the Korean War was a complex conflict involving multiple interests and impacts. While the U.S. intervention did stop the spread of communism in Korea, it also brought long-term division and turmoil to the Korean Peninsula.

American Student 3: Are you defending North Korea's aggression?

Shu Xiaoping: I'm not defending North Korea. I believe we need to view history objectively and understand the positions and motivations of all parties involved.

American Officer: I'd like to share some thoughts. I believe the Korean War was a significant factor in the deterioration of Sino-American relations. The war caused immense casualties and suffering on both sides. Chinese leader Mao even lost his son, which sowed the seeds for future antagonism.

American Officer: After the war, China targeted domestic capitalist elements, confiscating their properties. The

United States imposed a comprehensive economic blockade on China, leading to China's isolation from the rest of the world.

[Shu Xiaoping looks at the officer with admiration and gratitude.]

[Scene Ends]

Serendipitous Encounter - The Convergence of Love and Peace

[**Location**] Café

[**Time**] 1987

[**Characters**]

- Shu Xiaoping
- American Officer

[**Scene Description**]

Shu Xiaoping and an American officer unexpectedly encounter each other in a café.

American Officer: Ms.Shu Xiaoping, hello.

Shu Xiaoping: Hello.

American Officer: I apologize for the comments made by my fellow American students in class today.

Shu Xiaoping: It's alright, I can understand their

perspective.

American Officer: I'm glad to have met you. You are a very insightful person.

Shu Xiaoping: Thank you.

They begin to converse and discover they have many common interests.

In the background, the café's television broadcasts news about the Space Shuttle Challenger explosion and the Chernobyl nuclear disaster.

Shu Xiaoping: The world is truly unsettled.

American Officer: Yes, we should work together to contribute to world peace.

They get to know each other and begin dating.

[**Scene Ends**]

[**Background Music**] Gentle piano music

[Scene 32 (1)]

The Challenge at Tiananmen Square

[**Location**] Beijing, Tiananmen Square, Early Morning of June 4, 1989

[**Scene Description**]

The scene shifts to Beijing's Tiananmen Square. A large number of protesters have gathered, holding signs and shouting slogans. The atmosphere is tense and emotionally charged.

The camera shifts again to the intersection at Muxidi in Beijing.

Li Fei holds his girlfriend's hand, anxiously watching to the west. A convoy of military trucks roars past, the soldiers on board are tense and alert, as if ready to respond to any situation.

As the convoy passes, some in the crowd attempt to stop them but are quickly halted by the police.

Suddenly, the situation spirals out of control. People begin throwing stones at the military trucks, forcing the police to take action. The scene descends into chaos.

The camera cuts back to Tiananmen Square.

Protesters clash with the police, the noise filling the entire square. The police attempt to disperse the crowd, but the protesters are determined to stay, resolutely voicing their demands.

The camera then shifts to the United States.

[**Scene Ends**]

[Scene 32 (2)]

The Wedding and Human Rights

[**Location**] Interior / Wedding Venue / 1989 / USA

[**Camera Shot**]

In the United States, at the wedding of Shu Xiaoping in the United States. Shu Xiaoping and her American military officer husband stand at the entrance, welcoming guests. Tang Long arrives with his beautiful girlfriend to attend the event. At the banquet, guests are enjoying a wonderful time.

Suddenly, a television broadcast shows footage of a political event in China, sparking some discussion among the guests. Some express concern and worry.

Shu Xiaoping, her military officer husband, and other guests get into a heated argument. She tries to defend the dignity of her country.

The American television broadcast shows international

leaders expressing concern over the actions of the Chinese government, calling for respect for human rights and democratic values.

The wedding continues, and the guests keep enjoying this special moment. Shu Xiaoping feels some internal conflict and unease, but she strives to maintain a smile, not letting her emotions affect the wedding atmosphere.

After the evening concludes, Shu Xiaoping and her husband return to their room. They sit together, quietly discussing their feelings and thoughts. They respect each other's positions and try to understand each other's perspectives.

[Scene 32 (3)]

Confessions and Embraces - The Night in Beijing and Emotional Release

[Visuals return to Beijing]

Night falls, and Li Fei and his girlfriend stand on the balcony of their home, gazing at the dim streetlights in the distance. The lights from a convoy of military trucks flicker far away. The distant sound of loudspeakers can be heard, broadcasting announcements of martial law. The streets are bustling with people, yet it feels eerily quiet near the university.

A nearby radio broadcasts an editorial: "The Chinese government's crackdown on peaceful protesters has drawn global condemnation. This action will have far-reaching implications for China-U.S. relations."

The couple feels a heavy weight in their hearts. They express their sadness and anger but refrain from taking extreme measures. They hold each other, trying to provide comfort to each other in the midst of the turmoil.

[**Scene transitions to**] The Berlin Wall falls and the dissolution of the Soviet Union and its former republics.

[**Key elements**] The hurried silhouettes of people on the streets, the flickering lights of the military vehicles in the distance, the voice of the editorial on the radio, and the emotional exchange between the couple.

[**Background music gradually rises**]

[Scene 33]

Farewell and Decision

[**Location**] Interior / Family Home / USA

[**Characters**]

- Shu Xiaoping
- Shu Xiaoping's Husband
- Tang Long

[**Scene Description**]

Shu Xiaoping, her husband, and Tang Long sit together in the living room, preparing to bid farewell to Tang Long as he plans to return to China. The television broadcasts reports on the Gulf War, interspersed with excerpts from Deng Xiaoping's Southern Tour speeches.

[**Dialogue**]

Shu Xiaoping: Tang Long, are you really determined to go back to China? I know China is undergoing reform and opening up, but you've built a good life here in the States.

Tang Long: Yes, I've made up my mind to return. I feel that I can make a greater impact on China's development.

Shu Xiaoping's Husband: But you know China's environment and system are very different from those in the US. You need to be prepared for the adjustment.

Tang Long: I understand. I will do my best to adapt and work hard.

[Background Music]

[Scene 34]

Anxieties Before Nightfall

[**Location**] Exterior / Hong Kong Street Scene / 1997

[**Scene Description**]

The camera pans over the nightscape of Victoria Harbour in Hong Kong, showcasing its dazzling array of lights. Tang Long has returned to China and makes a stop in Hong Kong to meet Li Fei.

At this moment, Hong Kong is on the cusp of its 1997 handover to China, and an air of anxiety pervades the atmosphere.

Li Fei and Tang Long drive along Hong Kong Avenue, witnessing the bustling night scene of the city—towering skyscrapers and busy traffic—yet they can also sense the uncertainty stemming from the political and economic climate as the handover approaches.

[Dialogue]

Li Fei: Tang, you finally came back!

Tang Long: Yes, I'm back!

Li Fei: The situation in Hong Kong is quite complicated right now. You need to be careful.

Tang Long: I know. I'll be cautious.

[Background Music in Hong Kong]

"Blue Lotus" and "Longing Little Ant"

The Intersection Before Hong Kong's Handover

[**Location**] Kwai Fong Bar, Hong Kong

[**Time**] 1997

[**Characters**] Tang Long, Li Fei

[**Scene Description**]

Lan Kwai Fong's bar street in Hong Kong is bathed in neon lights, bustling with shadowy figures. Tang Long and Li Fei sit at the bar, engaged in a low conversation.

[**Dialogue**]

Tang Long: I've decided to move to Shanghai.

Li Fei: Shanghai? There are plenty of opportunities there, but be cautious.

Tang Long: Don't worry, I'll be careful.

From the bar's television, a news broadcast can be heard:

Newscaster: Prime Minister Margaret Thatcher visits China and meets with Deng Xiaoping. The Sino-British Joint Declaration is signed. Chris Patten delivers his final policy speech.

Tang Long: Looks like the day of Hong Kong's handover isn't far off.

Li Fei: Yes, the future of Hong Kong is quite a mystery. We can only hope for the best.

The two share a moment of silence, then clink their glasses together.

Tang Long: Take care!

Li Fei: Take care!

After bidding farewell, they part ways. Li Fei heads to Hainan, while Tang Long goes to Shanghai.

[Background Music: Hong Kong's ambiance]

[Male Voiceover, Low and Reflective]

It was a time right after Deng Xiaoping's Southern Tour, a period of rapid economic development in Guangdong and Hainan. However, this boom also gave rise to rampant smuggling activities.

Li Fei was involved in the business of importing large-scale products, shipping steel from abroad to Hainan. Unscrupulous traders exploited the tax exemption policy for imported goods in Hainan by setting up fake projects to obtain duty-free import permits.

They would transport the goods to Hainan, clear them duty-free, then smuggle them to Zhanjiang Port in Guangdong, reaping enormous profits from tax evasion. The operation was extensive, involving a well-coordinated network including ports, customs, inspection agencies, transportation, and even law enforcement. The scale was unimaginable.

Initially, Li Fei was unaware of these activities, but he later witnessed everything and got entangled in it, narrowly escaping the clutches of local gangs, corrupt businessmen, and crooked law enforcement. With the help of friends, he managed to escape. Soon after, the notorious Lai Changxing smuggling case, which shocked the entire nation, erupted.

[Scene Ends]

[Scene 36]

Port Transfer

[Exterior: Hainan, 1998]

[Camera Shot] The camera gently sweeps over the beautiful landscapes of Sanya and Haikou, accompanied by a voiceover: The stunning vistas of Sanya and Haikou glisten under the tropical sun.

Li Fei disembarks from a plane and meets with local businessman Mr. Chen. After exchanging a few pleasantries, Mr. Chen warmly invites Li Fei to the port to inspect the goods.

Mr. Chen: Mr. Li, your several tens of thousands of tons of steel have arrived at the port and are being unloaded. The goods are piled up like a mountain. Rest assured, we've completed the customs procedures, and we'll be able to release the cargo soon.

Li Fei: Thank you for your hard work, Mr. Chen.

The group arrives at the port, where stacks of steel are seen piled high on the dock, with workers busily unloading.

Mr. Chen: Mr. Li, look, these are all your steel shipments.

Li Fei: Hmm, not bad.

Mr. Chen: The customs procedures are done; we can release the goods shortly.

Li Fei: Great, I'll leave it to you then, Mr. Chen.

[**Scene Music**] Light background music, or simply the sounds of the natural environment to enhance the atmosphere.

[Scene 37]

Enigmatic Night

[Interior: Opulent Karaoke Lounge, Night]

[Cut to] An opulent karaoke lounge, where Li Fei and Mr. Chen are seated in a private room, surrounded by beautiful female companions.

Li Fei: Mr. Chen, this cooperation has been very pleasant. Let me toast to you.

Mr. Chen: Mr. Li, you're too kind. I should be the one toasting to you.

The two clink glasses and drink heartily, the atmosphere is quite pleasant.

At this moment, an aide rushes into the private room and whispers to Mr. Chen.

Aide: Mr. Chen, there's a problem at the port. The goods have been detained by customs.

[Cut to] Mr. Chen has a change of expression, and Li Fei

notices something is amiss.

Li Fei: Mr. Chen, what's going on?

Mr. Chen: It's nothing, just a minor issue. I'll have someone take care of it right away.

Li Fei: No need, I'll go check it out myself.

Mr. Chen: Alright, I'll go with you.

The two leave the karaoke lounge and head to the port.

[**Scene Music**] The dance hall music continues, its lively rhythm masking the turbulent undercurrents.

[Scene 38]

Customs Dispute

[**Location**] Interior/Customs/Daytime

[**Characters**]

- Li Fei (Customs Broker)
- Mr. Lai (Businessman)
- Customs Director
- Secretary

[**Scene Description**]

Li Fei and Mr. Lai arrive at the customs office. Mr. Lai is carrying a large bag and attempts to go directly into the Customs Director's office.

[**Dialogue**]

Mr. Lai: This small issue can be resolved by talking to the director. Are you familiar with him? No? You will be once we get in there.

Secretary: Hello, please make an appointment first.

Mr. Lai: I know the director; I need your help.

Without waiting for a response, Mr. Lai pushes past the secretary and barges into the Customs Director's office.

Mr. Lai: Director Fang, hello!

Customs Director: And you are?

Mr. Lai: You don't know me; I'm Mr. Lai. I need your help; my shipment has encountered some issues at customs, and I heard you could assist me.

Customs Director: You should follow the proper procedures to resolve this.

Mr. Lai places the large bag on the table, unzips it, revealing bundles of new Hong Kong dollars.

Mr. Lai: I appreciate your attention, Director.

He then leads Li Fei out of the office.

Li Fei (surprised): You sorted it out? You don't even know him?

Mr. Lai: It's fine; now we know each other. The goods will be released tomorrow.

Li Fei: Wait, Mr. Lai, the payment hasn't arrived yet.

Mr. Lai: Here's the thing, the payment for this shipment is via a letter of credit from the Maple National Bank, and it will take some time to clear. Can you make an exception and release the goods now?

Li Fei: No, that's against the rules. Regardless of the bank, payment must be made according to the contract terms before the goods are released.

Mr. Lai: What should I do then? My goods are urgent and can't be delayed any further.

Li Fei: You could go to the bank and apply for a letter of credit negotiation; that way, you can get the payment more quickly.

Mr. Lai: But that would be too cumbersome and would incur extra fees.

Li Fei: There's no other way. If you use illegal means to release the goods, you could be breaking the law.

Mr. Lai (thinking): Alright, I'll think of something else.

Li Fei: Yes, it's best to follow the regulations.

Narrator: Li Fei didn't realize that this shipment would plant a hidden danger for him.

[**Scene Ends**]

[Scene 39]

Underlying Currents

[Exterior/Port/Night]

[Sound Effects] Waves crashing against the shore, a distant horn.

[Scene]

Night falls, the port is brightly lit, and massive cargo ships are docked at the pier. Li Fei receives a mysterious phone call. A low, ominous voice on the other end informs him that Lai's people have bribed port officials and stolen his cargo.

Li Fei (shocked): What?! That's impossible!

Voice (with a sinister laugh): You'd better get to the port quickly, or your cargo will disappear forever.

Li Fei (hanging up, face grave): Damn it!

[Scene] Li Fei rushes to the port, only to find the cargo already gone. Realizing the severity of the situation, he decides to report it to the police.

Police Officer (in black uniform and sunglasses): Mr. Li, please explain the situation in detail.

Li Fei (anxious): Someone has stolen my cargo, worth tens of millions of dollars!

Police Officer (calmly): Don't worry, we will investigate and apprehend the culprits as soon as possible.

[**Scene**] The police swiftly launch an investigation, pursuing the thieves on charges of grand theft. Meanwhile, Li Fei receives threats from the perpetrators, demanding his life as the price.

[**Voiceover, low and reflective**] This was Li Fei's working environment, filled with danger and challenges. Yet, he steadfastly adhered to his principles, undeterred by powerful forces, and bravely fought back.

[**Voiceover, narrative**] In those years, the Maple National Bank initiated import loan services in China via letters of credit, but due to a lack of understanding of Chinese law, billions of dollars in loans were left unprotected, resulting in total loss. The bank had to withdraw from China.

Many high-ranking officials in Chinese state-owned enterprises exploited this loophole, embezzling vast sums from the Canadian bank. Numerous private companies also defaulted on their debts, amassing their initial capital, including some now well-known publicly listed companies.

Li Fei also secured a substantial loan amount at that time. However, to maintain his integrity and not put his friends working at the bank in a difficult position, he went to great lengths to repay the loan, ultimately ending up with nothing.

[**Scene**] Time swiftly moves to 1998. Smuggling activities have become increasingly rampant, reaching a frenzied state. Li Fei senses that something significant is about to happen.

[**Sound Effects**] Music grows tense, foreshadowing an imminent storm.

[**Scene Ends**]

[Scene 40]

Escaping Danger

[Interior/Night/Hotel Room]

[Sound Effects]

Television broadcasting scenes and sounds from the Hong Kong handover, telephone ringing.

Li Fei is seated on the sofa in his hotel room, watching the grand ceremony of Hong Kong's handover. His expression is grave, with his eyes fixed on the screen as if lost in thought.

Suddenly, the telephone rings, breaking the silence in the room. Li Fei picks up the phone, and a friend's anxious voice comes through the receiver:

Friend: "Li Fei, run! You might be in danger!"

Li Fei: "What's happening?" Li Fei's heart races.

Friend: "The smuggling operation has been exposed. Those people have bribed customs and the police.

They're coming to arrest you and your partner. They might even kill you to silence you and frame you for the smuggling charges. You need to leave, now!"

Li Fei grips the phone tightly, beads of sweat forming on his forehead. He knows his friend is telling the truth; if he doesn't leave immediately, his life is at serious risk.

Li Fei: "I'm heading to the airport right now." He hangs up the phone, quickly gathers his belongings, and leaves the room.

[Scene 41]

Approaching Crisis

[Exterior/Train/Boat]

[Sound Effects] The sounds of a car driving, a train whistle, and waves crashing against the hull of a boat.

Li Fei and his partner, with the help of friends, escape Guangdong by car under the cover of night. Along the way, they are filled with dread, fearing detection by the pursuing police.

To evade capture, they make their way to the coast, rent a fishing boat, and flee into the vast open sea.

[Voiceover]

The smuggling plot failed completely, exposing the entire scheme. Smugglers, customs officials, and corrupt police officers were all apprehended. This shocking Zhanjiang "9898" smuggling case soon led to the even larger Lai Changxing smuggling scandal. The harrowing experiences, coupled with the internal power struggles within state-owned enterprises, left Li Fei disillusioned and he began to consider the idea of immigrating.

[**Canada/USA/1999**]

[**Sound Effects**]

The sounds of a city street.

Li Fei stands on a street in Canada, taking in the unfamiliar surroundings with a heart full of mixed emotions.

He has finally left behind the place that brought him so much pain and has embarked on a new life.

[**Voiceover**]

Li Fei started a new life overseas. How will he confront the challenges that lie ahead? What does the future hold for him?

[Scene 42]

Nostalgia in a Foreign Land

[**Camera**] Li Fei drives his car, with iconic North American landmarks and beautiful scenery flashing by outside the window.

[**Plot**] In 1999, Li Fei immigrated to North America, embarking on a tranquil new chapter of his life. He travels across the North American continent, witnessing the excellent living and working conditions abroad, which profoundly moves him but also leaves him somewhat bewildered. The camera captures scenes of XWave and SinoFox going public on the New York Stock Exchange and NASDAQ.

[**Background Music**] Popular music from the United States and Canada in the year 2000, including:

- Britney Spears - "Oops!...I Did It Again"
- Christina Aguilera - "Genie in a Bottle"
- Backstreet Boys - "I Want It That Way"
- NSYNC - "Bye Bye Bye"
- Shakira (Canadian pop star) - "Whenever, Wherever"

[Scene 43]

A Night in the City of Sin

[**Setting**] Interior, Las Vegas, 1999

[**Shot**] The dazzling nightscape of Las Vegas flashes by. Li Fei, feeling directionless, arrives in the city seeking relaxation and entertainment.

[**Plot**] At this moment, Li Fei encounters his American classmate, Shu Xiaoping, who is vacationing here with her husband, as well as another classmate, Tang Long. Tang Long has made a name for himself in Shanghai, becoming a prominent businessman in the area. He has been linked with numerous entrepreneurs and is dubbed a "business elite." His company is thriving, and he frequently travels to Macau and Las Vegas for vacations.

[**Setting**] Inside the casino, Tang Long and Li Fei, along with others, enjoy the performances and admire the beautiful architectural scenery.

[**Background Music**] Select neutral background music, such as the following:

- Michael Bublé - "Feelin' Good"
- Sade - "Smooth Operator"
- George Michael - "Careless Whisper"
- Michael Bublé - "Sway"

[Scene 44]

Reunion and Farewell

[Interior / Bar / Las Vegas]

After many years, university classmates Shu Xiaoping, Li Fei, and Tang Long reunite in Las Vegas. The excitement is palpable as they meet again. Joined by Shu Xiaoping's military officer husband, the four of them indulge in drinks at the bar, reminiscing about the old days. The atmosphere is lively and full of warmth.

As the drinks keep flowing, their spirits also begin to lift. They banter and laugh heartily, as if transported back to their university years. The military officer husband of Shu Xiaoping, usually reserved, also relaxes unusually and mingles effortlessly with the trio.

After several rounds of drinks, the four are in high spirits. Shu Xiaoping and Li Fei engage in light-hearted conversation, while Tang Long takes a moment to close his eyes and rest. Shu Xiaoping's husband appears slightly inebriated but still remains alert.

[End of Scene]

[Scene 45]

Urgent Mission

[Interior/Hotel/1999/LAS VEGAS]

Late at night, Shu Xiaoping and her officer husband return to their hotel room. Shu Xiaoping is completely inebriated, lying on the bed and snoring. Her husband gently removes her shoes and coat, tucks her in, and then heads to the bathroom to freshen up.

Suddenly, the officer's phone rings. He answers it, and a frantic voice comes through the receiver:

Voice: "Sir, there's an emergency at the Yugoslav embassy. You need to report to the Pentagon immediately."

The officer's expression changes drastically. After hanging up, he quickly gets dressed and leaves the hotel.

[Scene 46]

Diplomatic Crisis

[**Location**] Interior / Pentagon / Washington D.C.

[**Time**] 1999

[**Characters**]

- The husband of Officer Shu Xiaoping (American)
- General (American)
- Lu Cheng (Chinese)

[**Plot**]

Shot 1: Aerial view of the Pentagon, the camera gradually zooms in, transitioning into the interior of the Pentagon.

Shot 2: The General is seated at his desk, his expression solemn. Officer Shu Xiaoping's husband stands before him, visibly upset.

Officer Shu Xiaoping's Husband: "General, I can't believe this was a mistake! How could the Chinese Embassy be hit by a precision-guided bomb? This is no accident!"

General: "I understand your feelings, Colonel, but our investigation has confirmed it was indeed an accidental strike."

Officer Shu Xiaoping's Husband: "A mistake? How is that possible? Is your intelligence system that unreliable? Or did you deliberately target the Chinese Embassy?"

General: (Silence) "I can only stay aligned with the President's stance."

Shot 3: General: "Execute the order." The Colonel picks up the phone and begins to contact the Chinese military.

Shot 4: The scene shifts to the Ministry of Defense in Beijing. Lu Cheng is working in his office. The phone rings, and he answers it.

Lu Cheng: "Hello, this is the Chinese Ministry of Defense, Lu Cheng speaking."

Colonel: "Hello, Lu Cheng. This is the Pentagon. On behalf of the U.S. government, I would like to express our sincere apologies for the accidental bombing of the Chinese Embassy in Yugavia."

Lu Cheng: (in a cold tone) "We have received your apology.

However, we cannot accept the term 'accidental.' This incident has caused severe consequences, and we demand a thorough investigation and appropriate compensation for the victims.

Shot 5: The scene shifts to a television screen. U.S. President Bill Clinton is delivering a televised speech, apologizing to the Chinese people.

[**Narrator**] "On May 7, 1999, NATO, led by the United States, bombed Yugoslavia, resulting in the bombing of the Chinese Embassy, killing three Chinese journalists. This incident shocked the world and deeply wounded the hearts of the Chinese people.

[**Location**] Beijing / Ministry of Defense

[**Time**] 1999 - 2014

[**Characters**] Lu Cheng

[**Plot**]Lu Cheng, after graduating from a military university, returned to Beijing to work at the Ministry of Defense and eventually rose to the rank of senior colonel. Throughout his military career, he experiencing the embassy bombing, the U.S.-China EP-3 incident, the

Hong Kong garrison handover, 9/11, the Taiwan Strait crisis, and the Diaoyu Islands dispute, and witnessed corruption within the military leading to the downfall of Xu Caihou and Guo Boxiong. His confrontations with Officer Shu Xiaoping's husband are a recurring theme throughout the film.

[**Narrator**] "Lu Cheng witnessed the trials and tribulations of the Chinese military over the past two decades and experienced the ups and downs of U.S.-China relations. His story is also a reflection of the Chinese military and China's rise."

Crisis Confrontation

[**Location**] Interior / Air Force Headquarters / Beijing / 2001

[**Characters**] Lu Cheng, American Military Officer

[**Plot**] At the Air Force Headquarters, an emergency arises due to a U.S.-China aircraft collision incident. Lu Cheng negotiates with the American military officer.

[**Shots**]

1. The American military officer arrives in China, where Lu Cheng receives him.

2. Lu Cheng engages in a verbal exchange, arguing persuasively based on facts and principles.

3. Footage of the aircraft being dismantled and transported back.

[**End of Scene**]

[Scene 48]

Memory of 9/11

[**Location**] Interior / Hotel / 2001

[**Characters**] Lu Cheng, American Officer Thomas

[**Plot**] One morning, Lu Cheng hurriedly knocks on the door of American Officer Thomas's hotel room.

[**Shots**] Thomas opens the door, astonished to see Lu Cheng's anxious expression.

Lu Cheng: (Panicked) Thomas, you need to turn on the TV. Something terrible has happened!

Thomas: (Confused) What happened?

Lu Cheng: (Pointing to the TV) Turn on Phoenix TV, quickly!

Thomas turns on the TV. A shocking news report about the 9/11 attacks appears on the screen.

[Screen: The TV news shows footage of the attacks on the World Trade Center.]

Thomas: (Stunned) This... This can't be happening...

Lu Cheng notices a photograph on the table and recognizes a familiar face.

Lu Cheng: (Heart sinking) This person is...

Thomas: (Anxious) She's at the World Trade Center...

Lu Cheng: (Resolutely) Let me help you find her.

Lu Cheng uses his connections to help Thomas get in touch with his wife. On the phone, Thomas hears his wife's voice, choked with emotion.

Thomas: (In tears) I'll come back as soon as I can. Everything will be alright.

Lu Cheng quietly exits the room, leaving Thomas alone with his wife on the phone, his own heart heavy with turmoil.

Scene 48

(Additional Scene)

[**Plot**] United States launches an attack on Iraq, marking the onset of the Second Gulf War.

[**Shots**] Television screen—International news reports rapidly flash by, covering the situation in Iraq, parliamentary debates, and footage of global protests.

[**Background Music**] Suspenseful and tense score.

[Scene 49]

Friendship and Downfall

[**Location**] Interior / Sanlitun / Beijing / 2008

[**Shots**]

A sweeping shot captures the vibrant scenes of the 2008 Beijing Olympics. Li Fei, Shu Xiaoping, and Lu Cheng reunite in Beijing. They tour Beihai Park, then head to the lively bar street in Sanlitun for a night of drinking.

Li Fei invites Shu Xiaoping and Lu Cheng to watch the lighting of the Olympic torch at the café of the Pangu Seven Star Hotel. Brilliant and vibrant fireworks illuminate the Bird's Nest, Water Cube, and Niangniang Temple.

They discuss the news of Tang Long's rapid rise in Shanghai, sharing their mixed feelings.

Suddenly, they receive shocking news: Tang Long has been indicted by the Shanghai Public Security Bureau and the Procuratorate for alleged foreign exchange fraud.

[Background Music]

[Shanghai / 2009]

The dazzling nightscape of the Shanghai Bund. Li Fei and Shu Xiaoping rush to Shanghai, hoping to help Tang Long, but their efforts prove futile. In court, they witness Tang Long receiving a seven-year prison sentence.

Narrator:

After his release, Tang Long was expelled from school. With the help of relatives, he studied abroad in the U.S., earning a master's degree.

After bidding farewell to Shu Xiaoping in the U.S., he returns to China and ventures into business in Shanghai. Thanks to his striking appearance and eloquence, he quickly becomes a prominent figure in Shanghai, rumored to have relationships with several Hong Kong and Taiwanese celebrities. His company's stock goes public in Shanghai, making him immensely wealthy. Tang Long frequently visits casinos in Macau and Las Vegas for high-stakes gambling. Eventually, he is convicted again for fraud and other crimes, receiving another seven-year prison sentence.

Narrator:

Tang Long's company's stock, "Tech," subsequently plummeted, leading to bankruptcy and was dubbed the worst A-share in China's history. To this day, Tang Long remains in prison.

[Scene 50]

The Moment of Judgment

[**Location**] Interior / Courtroom

[**Characters**] Li Fei, Shu Xiaoping, Bailiff, Tang Long, Lu Cheng (voice on the phone)

Li Fei and Shu Xiaoping stand in the courtroom, witnessing the verdict on Tang Long. The bailiff escorts Tang Long into the courtroom. The trial begins, and the verdict is announced. Tang Long is handcuffed and led out of the courtroom. Meanwhile, Li Fei's phone rings; it's a call from Lu Cheng. The news is grim. Lu Cheng: "Li Fei, I have bad news. Du Xiong couldn't bear the torture in prison. He escaped but was captured in the desert and died while being transported back."

[**End of Scene**]

[Scene 51]

Despair's Abyss

[**Location**] Interior / Prison / Xinjiang / 2010

[**Characters**]

- Li Fei (on the plane)
- Du Xiong (in prison)
- Prison Guards

Li Fei sits on the plane with his eyes closed, trying to relax. Lu Cheng's voice narrates in the background.

Lu Cheng (Voice-over): "Du Xiong is subjected to unjust treatment in prison. Day after day, he suffers through the hardships and torment within those walls. His mood grows increasingly heavy, filled with despair about the future."

[**Plot**] The scene transitions to the prison yard. Du Xiong is being brutally treated by the prison guards. His eyes burn with fury, yet he is powerless.

Lu Cheng (Voice-over): "Finally, Du Xiong could bear it no longer. He resolved to find other ways to assert his rights."

[**Scene**] It's late at night. Du Xiong seizes an opportunity when the guards are distracted. He stabs a guard to death and escapes the prison.

[**Background Music**] Tense and oppressive music underscores the scene.

[Scene 52]

Escape and Tragedy

[**Location**] Exterior / Desert / Xinjiang

Du Xiong, after escaping from prison, struggles to cross the vast desert. He is parched and exhausted. As he stumbles through the desert, he is spotted by the pursuing police officers.

[**Scene**] The police tie Du Xiong to the tail of a horse and drag him back.

Lu Cheng (voice-over): Du Xiong died after being captured during his escape in the desert.

[**Background Music**] Sad and desolate music

The scene shifts back to Beijing.

[**Scene**] Li Fei snaps out of his reverie. He gazes out of the window, his expression filled with complexity.

[**Narration**] Du Xiong's story leaves Li Fei in deep thought. He begins to ponder how he should choose his own path in life.

[Scene 53]

Memories Like Smoke

[**Location**] Interior / Xiangshan / Beijing / 2017

The film cuts back to a reunion scene in 2017.

[**Plot**]A courier delivers a letter, confirming that Du Xiong has passed away.

The atmosphere becomes heavy, interrupting Li Fei's thoughts. The scene shifts back to the class reunion.

Daughter walks in: "Dad, you seem upset. What happened? I saw that letter."

You mentioned him before. He made many mistakes and died trying to escape. But everyone makes mistakes, including you, Dad. Sometimes, changing our fate happens in an instant."

Daughter: "You made mistakes when you were young too. Tell me about them.

Li Fei lowers his head, unable to meet his daughter's

gaze. After a brief hesitation, he slowly says:

"That was before I married your mother. A friend and I decided to experience single life one more time." Daughter: "Looking back now, that doesn't seem quite right."

Shu Xiaoping walks over, breaking their conversation. "What are you two discussing?" She hands over a China Post package. "This just arrived. Tang Long has been released and has gone straight back to the United States." Li Fei feels a sense of relief, invigorated by the news of Tang Long's release.

Several classmates gather around, joyfully watching their children, faces beaming with happiness. "We've grown old. The children are the hope for the future, and they are happy. They don't know the poverty we experienced as kids, nor do they have our childhood experiences and innocent joys."

At this moment, the music abruptly stops, and the background TV screen starts broadcasting news.

"The nation is actively combating corruption. The government has announced a series of anti-corruption measures, emphasizing the rule of law."

Everyone watches the TV screen intently, their expressions serious. The news reports on various domestic political developments.

"Several government officials have been sentenced for violating the law."

Against this backdrop of news, everyone falls into deep thought, pondering the future of the country and the state of the world.

[Scene 54]

Unexpected Event

[**Location**] Exterior / Banquet Hall Entrance

A uniformed police chief walks into the banquet hall. The crowd moves forward to greet him.

Police Chief: "Classmates, I apologize! Due to an unexpected stability operation, I can only take a moment to meet with you all."

The crowd gathers around, shaking hands and exchanging pleasantries.

[Scene 55]

Farewell and Duty

[**Location**] Exterior / Foot of Xiangshan

A military-plate jeep drives into the banquet hall's courtyard. A soldier steps out of the jeep and hands a letter marked "Confidential" to Colonel Lu Cheng.

Lu Cheng opens the letter and, after reading it, addresses his classmates: "Classmates, I'm afraid I must leave now. I have just received an urgent notification from my superiors. Recently, U.S. fighter jets have been frequently approaching our South China Sea airspace for reconnaissance. To prevent any unexpected incidents, we need to strengthen our airspace surveillance."

The classmates express their understanding and support to Colonel Lu Cheng, shaking hands and waving farewell to one another. The military vehicle drives slowly away into the distance.

At that moment, a Chinese courier handed Li Fei an express delivery. Upon opening it, he found it to be the final judgment from the court, concerning his equity dispute with a certain cement conglomerate. The judgment confirmed that Li Fei held a 20% equity stake in the company (currently valued at 200 million RMB), but that after multiple transfers, the equity had been acquired by a state-owned enterprise. Due to the ambiguity of the original plaintiffs, the court dismissed Li Fei's appeal.

This was a result Li Fei had anticipated. After five long years of litigation, traversing multiple levels of the court system, Li Fei had witnessed firsthand the complexity and challenges inherent in the judicial process. The journey had been as dramatic and unpredictable as a film.

Despite this, Li Fei found a measure of solace in the fact that the judgment had confirmed the authenticity of his equity.

However, he was well aware that a legal battle against a state-owned enterprise would be even more arduous, with slim chances of success. Nevertheless, Li Fei was not one to give up easily. He resolved to continue his appeal and defend his legitimate rights.

Gazing into the distance, Li Fei knew the road ahead would be long and arduous. Yet, he was determined to press on, embracing the uncertainties of the future.

[Scene 56]

A Precious Goodbye

[**Location**] Capital Airport / Departure Lounge

Li Fei, Shu Xiaoping, and their classmates who came to see them off, including Lu Cheng, bid farewell to each other one by one.

[Scene 57]

Reunion and a New Era

[**Location**] New York, JFK Airport

Shu Xiaoping's husband, along with their child, warmly welcomes her and Li Fei. They embrace, celebrating the successful class reunion. Shu Xiaoping is overwhelmed with excitement.

The airport TV is broadcasting news:

1. CNN: "U.S. President Donald Trump appoints far-right figure Steve Bannon as Chief Strategist."

2. FOX: "President Trump to meet with visiting Chinese President Xi Jinping at Mar-a-Lago."

3. CNBC: "Russian President Vladimir Putin takes action on the Crimea issue, drawing international attention."

4. BBC: "Entrepreneur Elon Musk announces the successful launch of a rocket for the Mars mission; Tesla to unveil the Cybertruck electric pickup."

5. Voice of America: "An important interview is coming up."

The last piece of news catches Li Fei's attention.

[Music begins playing]

[Subtitles unfold... END]

[Background Music]

On-screen text appears, and a voiceover begins: "The main characters in this film are based on fictional stories. As time marches forward, dreams continue, and life will always move ahead..."

[Film Highlights]

1. The background music throughout the film (including scenes in China, the U.S., Canada, and Hong Kong), as well as songs and dances, should reflect distinct characteristics of their respective eras, being both popular and widely recognized.

2. Character dialogues should be concise; dialogue should be kept to a minimum unless absolutely necessary. Some scenes require no dialogue, with simple narration provided by the voiceover.

3. Certain scene shots should showcase famous landmarks, picturesque scenery, and broad vistas, reflecting both old and new, and highlighting clear characteristics of different eras.

4. The film should have a tight narrative, avoiding unnecessary details. Be it dialogue, fight scenes, or storytelling, the pace and rhythm should be strong and fast.

5. Filming locations: Beijing, Shanghai, Guangzhou, Shenzhen, Hainan, Hong Kong, Las Vegas, Washington, Canada. Numerous cities mean a high budget.

6. Chinese dialogue, English subtitles, with translation accuracy required.